THE JEWS IN OKLAHOMA

by Henry J. Tobias

Oklahoma Image is a project sponsored by the
Oklahoma Department of Libraries
and the Oklahoma Library Association,
and made possible by a grant from the
National Endowment for the Humanities.

Library of Congress Cataloging in Publication Data

Tobias, Henry Jack.
  The Jews in Oklahoma.

  (Newcomers to a new land)
  Bibliography: p.
  1. Jews in Oklahoma—History.   2. Oklahoma—Ethnic re-
lations.   I. Title.   II. Series.
F705.J5T62   976.6'004'924   79-6723
ISBN 0-8061-1676-5

CONTENTS

To Ann, Heidi, and Ruth,

whose lives add so much joy to

my own

PREFACE

The history of the Jews in Oklahoma, like that of all other groups which have settled there, draws together the collective and individual experience of the Jewish settlers and the conditions they encountered in their new place of residence. The historian then seeks to discover how these settlers adapted to these conditions to create an Oklahoma Jewish community. As a matter of formal study, the subject matter is virtually new. Outside of one published thesis completed in 1946 and one much briefer survey, little attention has been paid to it.

This effort is also a preliminary investigation, but the author hopes that it will provide some value to those who know nothing of the subject and have perhaps wondered about it from time to time. It may also provide some guidelines and directions for those who wish to study the subject more intensively.

The materials about the Jews in the state are poor. No collection on a state-wide or even community-wide level exists at this time and only a few industrious individuals have sought to maintain or keep some papers. Public materials exist for some periods on some subjects. Such conditions present the researcher with problems of documentation that severely limit the nature of the answers to questions put.

There is a brighter side of the question, in the willingness of those knowledgeable through life's experience and memory to aid the historian in his task. Oral materials of history, no less than written materials, require a critical eye. The personal encounter of the historian and his sources, however, provides a unique persuasiveness. The living sources can respond to questions as the written sources cannot. Those living contributors have been an essential part in the completion of this work.

Among those who have given of their time and information, I must thank the following persons: in Oklahoma City, Mrs. Erwin Alpern, Mr. Paul Byers, Mrs. Adeline Fagin, Mrs. Emma F. Friedman,

Mrs. Rose Grad, and Mr. Milton May; in Tulsa, Mrs. Jenny Brouse, Mrs. Yolanda Charney, Rabbi Arthur Kahn, and Mr. Nathan Loshak. In addition, the dedication and kindness of Mrs. Marian Saxe of the *Tulsa Jewish Review* have been noteworthy. I owe a special debt to Rabbi Levenson, formerly of Temple B'nai Israel and now living in Tallahassee, Florida, and Rabbi Randall M. Falk, formerly of Temple Israel of Tulsa and now in Nashville, whose earlier work aided me greatly and whose kind permission to use their work has been of great value.

A number of institutions have contributed the time of their staffs as well as their resources. At the University of Oklahoma, the Bizzell Library, the Western History Collections, and the Herbert Priestley Resources Center of the School of Journalism were all important. So were the Library of the American Jewish Committee in New York, the library of the Hillel Foundation at the University of Oklahoma and the library at Temple B'nai Israel in Oklahoma City.

My colleagues have been most understanding even though they bore the brunt of my constant quest for criticism and advice. Professor David W. Levy of the Department of History at the University of Oklahoma read the entire manuscript amidst his own time-consuming schedule as did Robert Rubin, the director of the Hillel Foundation. Rabbi A. David Packman of Temple B'nai Israel gave freely of his knowledge. My debt to all of them is a heavy one. The burden of any shortcomings, however, falls on my shoulders alone.

Not least of all, I owe my wife, Haven, a debt of gratitude for her criticism and patience when both were sorely needed.

University of Oklahoma   *Henry J. Tobias*

Chapter 1

THE JEWS AND IMMIGRATION

Jews have lived in America since the middle of the seventeenth century. They came to the New World for the same reasons which induced all other immigrants to come. Above all, that motivation was economic. In some instances, as in the case of the Irish in the mid-nineteenth century, the choice lay between emigration and starvation. More frequently the incentive was to gain better economic conditions rather than to escape absolutely intolerable ones. Jewish emigration, in different times and under varying conditions, fluctuated between the quest for a better existence and the desire to escape more drastic problems.

While not as important as economic reasons generally, political and religious motives also influenced people to seek refuge outside their homelands. The Irish, Poles, and Finns have all been affected by these considerations in modern times. For the Jews, too, particularly after 1880, political and religious factors contributed heavily to their desire to emigrate.

Jews shared in the conditions that confronted the societies in which they lived. In the nineteenth and twentieth centuries they emigrated when the general rate of emigration was high and stayed as the exodus abated. Common problems evoked common reactions. Nevertheless as a distinct people, the Jews were affected by and responded in their own way to the conditions which fostered emigration.

European Jews differed from the general population in some important respects. They formed a religious community separated by faith and traditions from the Christian majority. That circumstance helped to produce social attitudes and, at times, legal distinctions which partially isolated the two communities from each other. Unlike a large segment of Christian population, Jews engaged but little in agriculture. The occupational structure of Jewish economic activity leaned heavily toward commerce, manufacture, and artisanship. These activities, to a greater extent than with the remainder of the population, led the Jews to live in towns. As a result, an element of suspicion existed between themselves and the rural population. Furthermore, because of their distinctiveness, they often faced their Christian commercial and artisan counterparts in towns not merely as competitors, but as competitors of another kind.

Many of these distinctive traits dated from the Middle Ages. The dispersion of the Jews from the near eastern world in the wake of Islamic expansion had uprooted many of them from agricultural pursuits. Although no precise date can be fixed to determine when these occupations began to dominate Jewish life, the trend toward commerce, finance, and artisanship from the eighth to the eleventh centuries was unmistakable. As they entered the agrarian world of medieval western and central Europe the Jews, both by their own inclinations and those of the host society, could not reestablish themselves as agriculturalists.

European society, dominated by religious and feudal institutions which could not readily accommodate non-Christians, tended to keep Jews from the land and under the control of the political rulers. Only assimilation, expressed as conversion to Christianity, could significantly alter these conditions—a price Jews generally did not wish to pay. As a result, they lived in Europe under tenuous and insecure conditions protected by the church or kings under special rules designed for them, circumstances which insured a separate existence.

In any case, it was precisely their non-agricultural skills which made the Jews attractive as residents to the political rulers of Europe. The commercial and financial knowledge they had acquired and the network of contacts they had established among themselves made them valuable to the economies which they entered. They brought valuable artisan and trade skills to small towns bound to an agricultural society. If the Jews benefited at times from their relations to the ruling lords, their caste-like character also restricted their opportunity to achieve a social and economic profile which resembled the society in general.

Their religious and economic distinctiveness cost the Jews dearly in the long run. In difficult times they suffered the mark of the alien and the infidel. When people became enraged by economic dislocation and enthused by religious crusade the Jews lost their protectors.

2

They endured economic expropriation and physical expulsion. In the dislocation of the late Middle Ages migration again became a common experience for them and the centers of Jewish population shifted from western and central Europe to the eastern reaches of the continent.

By the sixteenth century the great Kingdom of Poland had become the chief residence of the European Jews. But the old distinctions followed them into the new centers. In the heavily agrarian economy of eastern Europe, where landholding remained the chief measure of honor and power, the Jews appeared in sharp contrast to the majority. And perhaps even more than in medieval western Europe their status as Jews and aliens kept them from agriculture. Still under the protection of kings and noblemen, they often served as middlemen and tax collectors between these political rulers and peasants and suffered their wrath whenever crisis struck the agrarian economy.

When Poland fell prey to the Prussian, Austrian, and, above all, to the Russian empires in the series of famous Partitions in the late eighteenth century, about half of the world's Jews became subjects of the Russian tsars. The well-established economic distinctions were perpetuated. The political and religious condition of the Jews, however, soon worsened under their new masters. The major difference from the past was that the Russian rulers did not act as their protector, but as a defender of the Christian population against them. Viewing them as a liability, the Russian state sought, sometimes simultaneously, to separate the Jews from the Christian population and to foster or even force assimilation.

In recent centuries the rise of the middle class, at the expense of traditional religious forces and old nobility, brought western and central European Jews economically and legally closer to membership in a single national community of citizens. But even that change did not erase the heritage of distinction. It outlived the enormous impact of secularization and egalitarianism which accompanied the rise of commerce and industry in the eighteenth and nineteenth centuries. And where the doctrines of the liberal emancipation movement encountered political reaction and economic dislocation, old attitudes quickly reasserted themselves. While western, and particularly, central European Jews faced age-old distinctions and attitudes in modernized societies, the eastern European Jews continued to live under conditions that reflected much of the older medieval traditions.

Nineteenth and twentieth century emigration to the United States from Europe took on epic proportions. In Europe, population pressures and economic change expressed in rural overcrowding, the misery of early industrialization, as well as oppressive political and religious policies, worked to uproot or encourage the departure to America of nearly 25,500,000 persons between 1820 and 1910. They did not come at an even pace or distribution, however, for Europe was no homogenous political and economic entity. The emigration appears rather as an ever-increasing wave with a gradual shift of emphasis in the migration from western and central to southern and eastern Europe.

Jews shared substantially in the emigration process. Between 1830 and 1924, when quota restrictions began to affect the flow, nearly 2,400,000 of them arrived. As a result of their exodus, the greatest in their history, the United States became a major center of Jewish residence.

The Jews came in two waves. The first, dating between the 1830s and the 1870s, with a peak in the 1840s and 1850s, emanated from central Europe. Jews departed from Bavaria, Poznan, and Bohemia in the wake of agrarian crisis and industrialization which dislocated peasant and artisan life. Their withdrawal coincided with the large non-Jewish emigration from these areas. Although precise figures do not exist, an estimated 50,000 Jews came to American shores during these decades.

The second wave, which began in the early 1880s, was tidal compared to the first. It was interrupted only by the disruption imposed by the conditions of World War I and the legal barriers introduced by the immigration legislation of the mid-1920s. The source of this migration was eastern Europe, particularly the Russian Empire, parts of Austria-Hungary, and Rumania. Between 1880 and 1914 alone nearly 2,000,000 Jews came to the United States. The Russian Empire gave up by far the largest numbers and, as in the earlier wave, Jews left together with considerable numbers of Poles and Finns.

The emigration from Russia resulted from dramatic changes in political conditions which followed upon the assassination of Tsar Alexander II in 1881. A series of pogroms, anti-Jewish riots, erupted, followed by administrative rules that materially changed the already difficult life of Russian Jewry. Long restricted by Russian law in choice of residence to the ghetto-like Pale of Settlement which was created out of the territories acquired after the Partitions of Poland

and a few other areas, the Jews now faced new and harsher limitations. The Russian state now excluded them from rural areas and small towns within the Pale itself with painful personal and economic effects. The state, furthermore, severely limited their opportunity to enter Russian gymnasia and universities as well as certain occupations by introducing restrictive quotas for the number of Jews who could be accepted.

The mass of Jews, some of whom had been cheered by the relatively liberal regime of Alexander II in the sixties, lost hope of ever achieving decent conditions in a society where few enjoyed them at best. For some, the only way out appeared in radical solutions. Zionism and the entry of Jewish youth into the revolutionary movement received strong impetus from the 1880s on. For most, however, the downturn in the state of their welfare under conditions which pressed them into already crowded cities where they faced lowered standards of living and outright poverty, the immediate solution became emigration to the United States.

Emigration from Europe on the scale of the nineteenth and early twentieth centuries was possible because of a historical coincidence —the simultaneous rise and development of the United States. Although the United States was hardly the sole receiver of immigrants, it was far and away the largest. Its size, relatively sparse population, and above all, its economic development and political conditions proved attractive to the dissatisfied, persecuted, and ambitious. In the latter decades of the nineteenth century Americans began to have misgivings about the unlimited entry of newcomers, particularly about those from Asia and, to a lesser extent, those from southern and eastern Europe. By and large, however, up to World War I, the United States appeared ready to accept all but the most unfit from Europe.

The more America developed the more attractive it became. Opportunity was so great that immigrants could almost count on improvement of their situation. Even in the last decades before the First World War, when the mass influx began to produce crowding in some areas, the new Americans sang the praises of their adopted country in letters to kin and friend in the old countries. So satisfied were they that they actually influenced the course of migration. "It is entirely safe to assert," the Dillingham report on immigration noted in 1910, "that letters from persons who have immigrated . . . have been the immediate cause of by far the greater part of the remarkable movement from southern and eastern Europe to the United

States. . . ."¹ The conjuncture of what made residence in Europe no longer tenable and the needs and promise of America which accepted immigrants readily made possible one of the great population transfers in history.

The Jews shared heavily in this optimism. The distressing reasons for their departure magnified their hopes for the future and reduced any chance of second thoughts. Memories of the old homeland could be bittersweet, but ideas of return only bitter. Perhaps more than any other large group of immigrants the Jews came to stay, bringing families with them and reemigrating only in small numbers.

Their history had made the Jews the most urbanized and trade oriented of all groups who came to these shores. In mid-nineteenth-century Prussia just over half of the Jews had engaged in trade and credit activity, and about 20 percent in handicrafts and industry. The Russian Jews of the second wave of immigration exhibited similar characteristics. The Russian census of 1897 found 74 percent involved in trade and manufacture (about equally divided), and only 3 percent in agriculture.

Their experience served the Jews well in their new environment. The timing of their migration from Germanic Europe in the middle decades of the nineteenth century coincided with the rapid expansion of the American economy and dispersion of population across the continent. Trade was a vital element in promoting and maintaining this growth and their strong disposition toward it placed these Jews on a major track of national economic development.

Before the American Revolution the few Jews who lived in the country had established communities along the eastern seaboard. Between 1840 and 1877, however, their numbers rose from 15,000 to 229,000. The central European Jews, who contributed significantly to that increase, did not cling to the coast, but participated in the westward movement. An unofficial census taken in 1880 located Jews in every state and territory except Oklahoma.² Although the pattern of their dispersion favored the northeast in receiving and holding newcomers, in 1877 more Jews lived in California than in any other state except New York. Missouri, just northeast of Oklahoma, with over 7,000 Jews, ranked ninth among the states and territories in its Jewish population.

The Jewish immigration between 1880 and 1914 dispersed in a markedly different pattern. The numbers involved, nearly 2 million, were so much greater than in the earlier period that increases in Jewish population occurred everywhere. The most noteworthy feature of the period, however, was the extraordinary growth of the New York Jewish community. In 1880 Jews made up only 3 percent of the city's population but in 1920 they formed 30 percent.[3]

This urban centered settlement resulted partly from the differences of background of the later immigrants. While commerce had dominated the activity of the central European Jewish newcomers, manufacture equaled commerce among the eastern European Jews. In 1900 one-third of the Russian-Jewish immigrants in New York worked in a single industry—clothing manufacture. The abilities of these immigrants and the opportunities at hand in the city combined to make New York and the industrial northeast more attractive than the distant and unknown west.

The heavy trend toward urban residence among Jews was scarcely unique. In Europe and America people were moving increasingly into cities. By 1910 the urban population of the United States (defined by the census as living in places with at least 2,500 persons) was 45 percent of the total. By 1930 the urban portion had reached 56 percent. But of the nearly 4,250,000 Jews in the country in 1927, fully 83 percent lived in cities of over 100,000. When the broadest definition of urban was applied, 97 percent of America's Jews were in cities.

The immigration process of the Jews to the United States duplicated their European occupational experience. They came and remained heavily committed to commerce and industry. The economic character of their population fit in well with the existing needs of American development. Their ability to transfer or adapt their skills and the receptivity of America to them, abetted by the social and political openness often absent in Europe, explains at least the basis of the generally satisfying experience of Jewry in the United States.

Chapter 2
SETTLEMENT AND LIVELIHOOD IN OKLAHOMA

Oklahoma's early development was set in the late 1820s and the 1830s with its creation as an Indian territory. After the Civil War it began to undergo rapid change. The building of railroads, the desire to exploit the resources of the area, and the insatiable land hunger of the ever-growing population of the United States all combined to impinge on the established usage of the Territory. Even in the last decade of the nineteenth century, however, Oklahoma was still a land of a few small towns, vast tracts of virginal lands, with only the beginnings of an extractive economy.

It was in this postwar period of dynamic change that Jews first arrived as settlers and community builders in Oklahoma. With their special background of trade and commerce they began to fill the gaps in the new markets which appeared as a result of the growing local population and expanding regional trade. Oklahoma appeared as a land of opportunity after the Civil War, and those willing and able to take risks and work hard could make their fortunes. The relatively open character of a new society lent incentive to persons who had not always met with ready acceptance in rigidly stratified social and economic orders.

Jewish settlement in Oklahoma began slowly. The raw and strongly rural character of life did not attract as many Jews as did other parts of the country. The Jewish population grew only as Oklahoma blossomed into a boom area after the Run of 1889 and statehood in 1907. Even then the growth of Jewish numbers remained small compared to those entering the country up to the Great Depression of 1929. Within the state the distribution of their settlement matched its development. They moved into small towns mainly in the eastern half and gradually became an urban population as Oklahoma's cities grew.

In economic terms, Oklahoma's Jews followed the major lines of their traditional experience. They came as peddlers and salesmen and, when opportunity and resources permitted, became shopkeepers. The range of their activities broadened as the nature of Oklahoma's economy changed. New industries, offering new opportunities, led the Jews to adapt their skills and investments.

As a small community, Jews related to the overwhelming majority with a mixture of caution and openness. Their paucity of numbers and the forms of their economic activity held them close to the neighboring population both out of desire and necessity. But their desire to maintain their identity led them to build a network of institutions to preserve and foster their traditions.

How many Jews lived in Oklahoma before the Run of 1889 is hard to determine. Given the absence of formal congregations or

Interior of the Lowenstein store, Apache, Oklahoma, 1908. Courtesy of Mrs. Molly Levite Griffis.

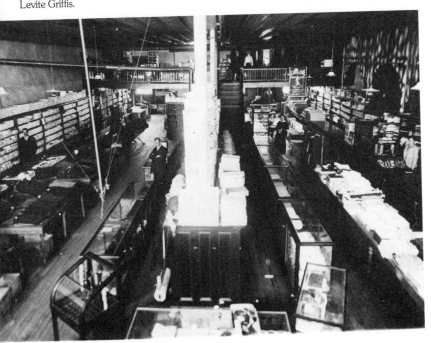

communal institutions before that date, it is not surprising that an 1880 survey found none. Those who resided in Oklahoma then did so as individuals or small family groups not readily identifiable to census takers. Nevertheless, there may have been as many as 100 in the Territory in 1890, half of them located in Ardmore.[1]

The number of Jews in the Territory increased markedly between the Run of 1889, which opened lands to non-Indian settlement, and 1907 when Oklahoma achieved statehood. An estimate made in 1901 by the *American Jewish Year Book* placed their numbers at one thousand.[2] The *Year Book* repeated that figure annually until 1910. Its continued use suggests the absence of new data rather than the actual state of affairs for a decade and the estimate is probably more accurate for the beginning of the decade than for its end. A private survey conducted by Rabbi Joseph Blatt of Oklahoma City, who arrived in Oklahoma in 1906, placed the number of Jews in the Territory at 1,200 in that year. In 1909 he calculated their numbers at about two thousand.[3] Even the *Year Book*'s modest unadjusted figure of 1,000 in 1907 meant a tenfold increase between 1890 and statehood.

By 1907 there were more Jews in Oklahoma than in seven western states and territories. Kansas to the north and Arkansas to the east, much older states, had 1,500 and just over 3,000 Jews respectively. Given the newness of Oklahoma's non-Indian settlement, the Jewish presence was promising.

Between statehood and the Great Depression Oklahoma's growth continued uninterruptedly. The state's population climbed from 1,400,000 to 2,400,000 from 1907 to 1930, a 70 percent increase compared to a 40 percent expansion for the whole population of the country. Its rank among the states, however, advanced only modestly, from twenty-third to twenty-first place.

During that period of expansion, Oklahoma's Jewish population grew at a faster rate than the state's total population. From the estimated 1,000 noted in the 1907 *Year Book* it had grown to about 7,800 in 1927—nearly an eightfold increase. Oklahoma's Jewish population ranked forty-second among the states in 1907. By 1930 it had climbed to thirty-first.

Even with this considerable growth, Oklahoma's Jews remained a tiny minority. Between 1907 and 1927 the Jewish share of the state's population rose only slightly, from 0.06 percent to 0.33 percent. Such an increase, while meaningful in terms of how Jews arranged their lives as a community, did not appreciably alter the ethnic or religious balance of the state's population.

10

In terms of regional growth, Oklahoma's Jews also did well. Jews in Kansas and Arkansas were more numerous than in Oklahoma in 1910, but all were virtually equal in 1930. Of the three states, Oklahoma's Jewish population grew the most rapidly during this period. Despite this favorable aspect of comparison, in none of the states mentioned did the Jews' share of the population reach one-half of 1 percent. Even Texas, with more favorable growth conditions, did not acquire a Jewish population of 1 percent. The increase in Oklahoma's Jewish population, thus, was in line with the regional Jewish growth rate.

The era of the Depression, World War II, and beyond, from 1930 to 1955, witnessed an absolute decline in Oklahoma's population. It fell from 2,400,000 to 2,210,000. Viewed from a national standpoint, the state's position was not a happy one, for the country's population continued to rise. As a result, Oklahoma's rank among the states dropped from twenty-first place to twenty-sixth.

Oklahoma's Jewish population also declined during this period. From a high of 7,800 in 1927 it fell to an estimated 4,750 in 1955, a greater rate of decline than that of the state's population. And like the nation's growth condition, the Jewish population also continued to grow. Under the circumstances, Oklahoma's rank in terms of Jewish population fell from thirty-first place in 1930 to thirty-sixth place in 1955, precisely the number of places dropped by the state.

As always, population data leave doubts about both decline and growth. The *Year Book* indicated a drop in Oklahoma's Jewish population between 1927 and 1940 from 7,800 to 7,300. But the more controlled data based on membership of Jewish congregations from 1926 to 1936 indicated a modest increase from 4,098 to 5,396. The number of congregations increased from nine to ten during that period.[4] Yet the membership of congregations may have grown while the total population of the Jews decreased.

It is impossible to identify the first Jewish settler in Oklahoma. An early effort at constructing the history of the Jews in the state, relying on secondhand information, mentioned the presence of a Bogy Johnson, who came to the Territory after the Civil War, married a woman of Chickasaw parentage, and settled in Atoka County. From then on, he apparently blended with his wife's people. The assumption of Johnson's Jewishness seems less than certain. Even if he were a Jew, his marriage outside the faith and the absence of any trace of Jewish activity or heirs left little to establish him as the founder of the history of the Jews in Oklahoma.

The story of Bogy Johnson forces us to consider the proper limits

11

of this investigation. Given the religious and ethnic nature of Jewish identity, persons not openly acknowledging that identity or, for whatever reasons, severely limiting their ties with Judaism or Jewry through lack of opportunity, slight interest, or absence of conviction, become marginal figures in the history of the Jews. Bogy Johnsons are found throughout the history of the Jews in many environments. The classic example is of the peddler striking off alone into frontier areas, cut off from contact with his fellow Jews, marrying out of the tradition, and raising a non-Jewish family. Such persons usually ended all but the most perfunctory attachment with the communal past, leaving little possibility of a Jewish future. To write the history of Oklahoma's Jews means to write primarily about how they have lived as Jews, that is, as a community that involved identity, numbers, and organization.

By contrast, other early Jewish settlers in the Territory left clear evidence for historical reconstruction. Their biographies disclose the economic and social patterns by which the first settlement of Oklahoma's Jews took place.

The career of Joseph Sondheimer, who became a merchant in Muskogee, is a case in point. Born in Bavaria in 1840, he came to the United States at the age of twelve, during the height of the central European immigration and lived in Baltimore with family friends from the old country. Later he moved to Pennsylvania where he managed a store, and from there he moved to St. Louis. When the Civil War broke out he set up stores and commissary stations at Memphis, Cairo, and other points. After the war, Sondheimer, seeing great potential for development in the Southwest, took a trip to the Indian Territory on horseback in 1866. His travels affirmed his hopes. Sondheimer opened several depots for hides and pecans along the military road from Fort Scott, Kansas, to Jefferson, Texas. He also established a warehouse at Muskogee, then scarcely a village, which became the distribution and shipping point for his goods. Although Sondheimer spent most of his time in the Territory from then on, the headquarters of his business remained in St. Louis until 1872. When the Missouri, Kansas and Texas Railroad, the "Katy," extended its tracks through the Territory, he moved his headquarters to Muskogee.

At about the same time he embarked on his ventures in Oklahoma, Sondheimer married in St. Louis. In 1878 or 1879 he brought his family to Muskogee and the two survivors of his five children grew up as permanent residents of the state. When he died in 1913

Henry J. Tobias

he was the oldest citizen of the town in years of residence as well as its pioneer merchant.[5] Joseph Sondheimer, unlike Bogy Johnson, raised his children as Jews and was himself interred finally in Mount Sinai cemetery in St. Louis.

The biography of another early arrival, Sam Daube of Ardmore, was similar. Born in Germany in 1859, Daube came to America in 1877. He located first in New York and struggled to earn a living. After several years he moved to Texas and in 1883 opened a general store in Bowie. Around 1885 he came to Ardmore (while retaining the store in Bowie) and in 1888 joined with his brother Dave and fellow townsman from Germany, Max Westheimer, to run the general store long known as Westheimer and Daube. In 1894 he married in Chicago and he and his wife returned to raise their children as permanent residents of Ardmore. Sam Daube died in 1946.[6]

Sondheimer's and Daube's experiences revealed one pattern of early settlement; movement from an established economic base to a new opportunity. They took up residences in the new locale without abandoning their businesses in the old. The experience of the Daube family, moreover, introduces another element into the picture of early Jewish settlement. Dave Daube came to Ardmore after a relatively short time in his newly adopted land. He joined his brother and Westheimer in residence and business, forming a nucleus which helped to promote the creation of a community.

Stories of other Jews who came before the Run of 1889, although few in number and skimpy in detail, confirmed these patterns. None of the early immigrants appears to have come directly from his port of entry to the Territory, although the length of residence involved before arriving in Oklahoma varied from a few months (in cases where family members had preceded them) to many years. The phenomenon of coming alone and establishing themselves economically before marrying also appears regularly, and the brides frequently were not Oklahomans. Economic opportunity, as for many other people, seemed to be the primary motivation for coming; suitability for family life and permanent settlement followed. The tempo and style of their approach to Oklahoma suggest a cautious and undramatic, if steady, advance.

While the earliest Jewish residents concentrated in Ardmore and to a lesser extent, Muskogee, after the land runs, newcomers began to move into the newly opened areas. By 1907 the largest concentration of Jews lived in Oklahoma City with a community of 275 persons. By then Ardmore had 100, while Muskogee also contained a sizable

13

group. The remaining two-thirds of Oklahoma's Jewish population, however, were scattered in about forty towns, mostly throughout the eastern half of the state.

The pattern of dispersion indicated that at least two factors were at work among the Jewish settlers. Their attraction to the larger population centers emulated their behavior in Europe and in the eastern United States; their skills and interests in commerce and manufacture drew them to cities. But the heavy influx of population into Oklahoma between 1889 and 1907 also contributed to the growth of many new small towns where opportunities for setting up commercial enterprises were great. A newcomer might readily establish himself with small capital investment and without facing stiff competition. Jews partook also of these opportunities.

Easier access, made possible by the introduction of new rail lines, the growth of markets, and better knowledge of the area, also account for the increased numbers of Jews. Ben Byers, an immigrant from the Russian empire who came to Oklahoma in 1891, worked at first as an agent for a photography company, traveling up and down the route of the "Katy" making stops at larger towns. In 1895 he went into the dry goods business at Checotah, stayed one year, and then relocated at Lehigh. Achieving some success, Byers, together with a business associate, Simon Levine, put in a branch store at Coalgate. Byers remained in business in Lehigh until 1920.[7]

The case of Martin Zofness, although dated shortly after statehood, is also instructive. Zofness arrived in the United States in 1906, an immigrant from Russia. Learning of statehood, he and his brother came to Oklahoma in 1910 to go into business, "a step of progress" in the minds of the young men. On the basis of his brother's tailoring experience, the two opened a store in Clinton, in western Oklahoma, but soon met with disappointment. They then relocated at Bartlesville, after Zofness' brother, upon reaching the town in the evening, was fascinated "by the glow from the smelting furnaces' fires...which was sufficient evidence of employment and prosperity."[8]

The stories of Byers and Zofness differed somewhat from the earlier pattern of settlement. They made no intermediate steps between their experience at the port of entry and their decision to come to Oklahoma. All immigrants sought to better their economic position, but in their search for upward mobility neither Byers nor Zofness possessed the relative economic advantages enjoyed by Sondheimer or the Daubes. The risks they took in the atmosphere

14

The Ben Byers store in Lehigh, Oklahoma, about 1916. Courtesy of Mrs. Adeline Fagin.

of growth of late territorial and early statehood days seemed well worth the effort.

While such examples of successful settlement are typical of the early period, evidence tends to survive for those who persevered and made a go of their efforts, if not on the first try, then on the second or third. Those who failed often left little or no trace; they simply moved on.[9] The question of how many successes there were compared to the failures must be left open.

Whether in small town or large, the character of the economic activity of the Jews moved along lines in keeping with their earlier experience or expectations. As soon as opportunity and their resources enabled them to do so, they opened stores, often in the clothing, dry goods, or hardware lines. A few moved into manufacture. In smaller towns they often chose some line of enterprise which was the only one of its type locally.

At the simplest level, single families or individuals settled in a town. The Levite family of Apache established a general store in 1903 and traded with the Indians. A single member of the Grad family

15

Interior of Levite's Handy Corner Store, Apache, Oklahoma, 1915. Courtesy of Mrs. Molly Levite Griffis.

in Carnegie ran the later well known Dixie store for many years after 1911 which also handled general merchandise. In larger towns greater diversity prevailed. Muskogee, the second largest city in the state in 1907 had Jewish merchants running general stores, dealers in hides and pecans, scrap metal dealers, grocers, pawnshop proprietors, insurance agents, and attorneys. Ardmore, with the second largest Jewish community at the same date, supported a similar range of activity with the addition of cotton marketing and cattle raising. In Oklahoma City, the largest city in the state with the largest Jewish population, some considerable duplication of enterprises owned by Jews had already grown up and even some specialization. Not only were there attorneys but even a county attorney; not one clothing store, but a number of them. In general, the larger the town, the greater was the variety of activities in which they engaged. The total range of their occupations, however, remained limited to commercial enterprises with a sprinkling of professionals.

In the long generation between statehood and the Great Depres-

Levite's Handy Corner Store, Apache, Oklahoma, 1903. Courtesy of Mrs. Molly Levite Griffis.

sion urban growth became an important feature of Oklahoma's economic development. The urban share of the population was just over 19 percent in 1910, but by 1930 it had risen to over 34 percent. Oklahoma City and Tulsa emerged as the major cities. In round figures, Oklahoma City grew from 64,000 to 185,000 in that generation, while Tulsa expanded from 18,000 to 141,000. In 1910 the two cities contained 25 percent of the state's urban population and about 5 percent of all Oklahomans. By 1930 they had acquired 40 percent of the state's city dwellers and nearly 14 percent of the entire population. From 1910 to 1920 the two centers accounted for 37 percent of the entire urban increase and from 1920 to 1930 they accounted for 57 percent of that growth. They not only increased their share of the state's population, but did so at an increasingly rapid rate.

By contrast, the smaller towns experienced uneven growth. New towns appeared and grew while older ones stabilized or declined. The earlier centers of Jewish settlement illustrated the pattern.

17

Ardmore, which had 8,700 residents in 1910 and 14,000 in 1920, barely reached 15,000 by 1930. Muskogee, with 25,000 in 1910, inched ahead to only 32,000 by 1930.

As the two major centers increased in size between 1907 and 1930 so did their Jewish population. Oklahoma City, with 275 Jews in 1907, contained 1,250 by 1927. Tulsa, whose Jewish population had attracted no attention for data collection in 1907, had passed Oklahoma City as the largest center of Jews in the state with 2,400 by 1927. The two cities alone accounted for 46 percent of the state's Jewish population just before 1930. The Jews clearly reiterated their urban preference to a greater extent than the population as a whole.

Outside of Tulsa and Oklahoma City, no town in the state accumulated a large Jewish population. Muskogee, third in rank in 1918, had 225 Jews. Ardmore, which had about 100 in 1907, had 150 in 1918. These were moderate increases, much like the growth of the towns themselves. A decade later estimates indicated decreases for both towns, with 200 Jews noted for Muskogee and only 67 for Ardmore. Okmulgee, which exhibited considerable growth up to 1920, reported a Jewish population of 125 in 1928, the only town outside the two large centers and Muskogee to register over 100 in that year. Beyond these few communities which counted 100 or more, the *American Jewish Year Book* of 1918–1919 noted the presence of 3,461 Jews in 131 small towns in Oklahoma.[10] In 1928 the same source listed 32 communities with between 10 and 99 Jews and 27 communities with fewer than 10. By contrast with Oklahoma City and Tulsa, the broad picture of Jewish settlement showed a lack of dynamic growth at best and a decline at worst.

Their traditions continued to dominate the Jews' selection of occupations in the period between 1907 and 1930. Their choices, even in this period of urban growth, still tended to complement rather than duplicate those of the majority. The coming of new immigrants from abroad and other parts of the country and the appearance of generational patterns did not alter their practices greatly.

Even in 1930, two-thirds of Oklahoma's population was rural. Before and after statehood the availability of land was a powerful factor in attracting and holding people. From 1900 to 1910 that impulse was extremely strong, the number of farms increasing from 108,000 to 190,000, a rise of some 76 percent. After that the number of new farms slowed dramatically, increasing only 1 percent by 1920 and about 3 percent more by 1925.

Few Jews were farmers. A survey of agricultural activity among

American Jews in 1913 noted only nine Jewish families farming in the state, with 1,365 acres in their possession. Nor did ranching attract any significant numbers. Sam Daube raised white-faced Herefords and apparently did quite well at it. One commentator noted that "in all Western markets where cattle are bought and sold, the name of Sam Daube is as well known as his brands."[11] An old-timer remembered Westheimer and Daube as "two Jews who owned thousands of acres of land and had thousands of head of cattle."[12] Jake Bodovitz of Ardmore, another early settler, also raised stock. In each of these instances the individuals also engaged in many other economic activities. Moreover, those who engaged in cattle raising were persons of considerable means who branched into the line after establishing themselves in other fields. Cattle raising also seemed limited to persons who lived in smaller cities. The Jews in ranching were fairly prominent and old-line members of the group, but were few in number.

While many small-town Jews did not participate directly in agriculture, their livelihoods were often linked with its general welfare. Alexander Grossman of McAlester, in the second decade of the century, dealt in cotton and ginning as the importance of that crop grew in the state. The Davidsons of Muskogee worked with cotton batting, while Sam Daube had engaged in cotton brokering before statehood. The Sondheimers from the first had dealt in pecans on a large scale as well as in wool. Where opportunities for marketing agricultural products appeared, Jews became involved. This was limited to the substantial smaller cities, rather than Oklahoma City or Tulsa.

Even where direct connections with agriculture were absent, the Jews, like all citizens in the small towns, were affected by the economic condition of agriculture. In the late twenties an economic survey of the state found that "though the petroleum industry has profoundly influenced the growth of numerous communities, most towns in Oklahoma are essentially the 'service stations' of the surrounding farm territory."[13] Even where mining was an important economic activity, its relation to the town could be marginal. By 1900 the coal miners of Oklahoma were highly specialized industrial workers living in a semi-self-sufficient agricultural region.[14]

Conditions after 1910 did not improve the prospects for growth of towns that depended on farming. As the number of farms ceased to grow, the need for new business outlets slowed and even declined in some places. Many factors contributed to the change of conditions in agriculture: mechanization and an increase in the size of individual farms, changes in crop prices influenced by world price structures, and the very nature of small-scale farming in Oklahoma with its heavy degree of tenancy. But none brought additional persons to farming. As a result the small towns dependent on the farm population tended to stay small or to languish.

A fair number of Jews, however, lived in the small towns between 1910 and 1930. The unfavorable conditions did not develop all at once and resettlement could be difficult. Favorable economic circumstances had often permitted long-term settlement. Those who had achieved some success and had raised their families in the towns had close links with the community. Often children would join or take over the family enterprise. Joseph Sondheimer's children, Alexander and Samuel, fully grown before statehood, stayed on in Muskogee in the lines of business pioneered by their father. Harris Handverker, who had settled in Lawton in 1901 and had built up a department store, was joined by his son Morris. There were numerous examples of this generational continuity, for it was not easy to set aside the work of a lifetime. The pride of passing the business on also gave satisfaction to both generations involved.

There were some variants of this continuity in the reasonably stable towns. Even where a family business did not continue, the second generation might stay on in the town and move into other lines of business. Max Davidson, who came to Muskogee from St. Louis in 1912 and opened a clothing store, did quite well. In 1922 the business burned, and although Davidson restocked, by 1928 he decided to return to St. Louis. His sons, however, moved into the jewelry business and stayed in Muskogee. The Kirschners, who had settled in Muskogee in 1905 and operated a clothing store, illustrated another adjustment. Phil Kirschner, a son, established his own business in 1916. In the twenties both father and son left the mercantile line and entered oil and real estate activities in Muskogee. People stayed in one locale from one generation to the next, making adjustments as fortunes and opportunities changed.

Generational continuity in the small towns was not the only pattern that developed. Educational opportunities, often absent for the first-generation immigrants and deeply desired for their children, allowed the second generation to pursue careers in other places. The sons of Jake Bodovitz of Ardmore became attorneys in Oklahoma City and Tulsa in the twenties. One daughter married in Ardmore and the other moved to New York. The Berty and Rose

Weitzenhoffer family, which settled at Purcell before the Run of 1889, underwent several variants of generational settlement. Their children moved to Oklahoma City, Los Angeles, and New York. The children of Morris and Sophie Schonwald, who lived in Tonkawa, also left their hometown. A daughter who married moved to Florida and a son, Fred Paul, moved to Oklahoma City to practice law. Such instances were fairly common. This pattern of second-generation exodus must to some extent account for the slowdown of Jewish growth in the small towns of Oklahoma.

The most dramatic changes in Oklahoma's economy between statehood and 1930 occurred around the rise of the petroleum industry. Although the presence of oil in the area was long known, new discoveries and uses for the product led to enormous increases in demand and output. In 1900, seventy-five hundred barrels were produced in Oklahoma. By 1910 production passed 50 million barrels and in 1916 that had doubled. In 1927 Oklahoma placed first among the states in production with over 276 million barrels. In terms of value of production, Oklahoma already ranked first by 1922.

The new discoveries created an economic revolution in the state. Many towns, particularly in the eastern half of the state, reflected the change. Coal mining towns, once so important in connection with the coming and running of the railroads, faltered badly. Lehigh's population, which was 1,800 in 1910, fell to 497 by 1930. Other towns experienced a sharp boom. Seminole, an oil center of large scale production in the twenties, grew from 854 in 1920 to 11,459 in 1930. Other towns, such as Blackwell, perhaps more diversified, showed moderate growth on the basis of the new industry. Some became centers for oil field operations. Businesses dealing in supplies for the oil fields and facilities for distribution and manufacture as well as offices for oil companies became a part of the Oklahoma scene.

For the Jews, as for the rest of the population, the effects of the boom were mixed. Those who lived in areas where discoveries were made at times could take advantage of the new opportunities. In Carter County, one field was named Sholem Alechem, the Hebrew phrase meaning "peace be with you." Harris Brenner, a post trader in Pawhuska at various times during the eighties and nineties, had foreseen some of the potential in oil. In 1902 he helped organize the First National Bank of Pawhuska and became its president. In 1903, he started the Pawhuska Oil and Gas Company. At that time there was no production within twenty-five miles of the town. Obtaining Indian land leases after 1904, the company did well and moved into leasing in other parts of the state. Dave Schonwald, after a variety of ventures in Blackwell, became interested in the Kay County and Three Sands oil fields in 1915. With friends, he organized the Security State Bank and developed Harold Petroleum and Kay Oil. Jews thus benefited in some cases from the boom in the small towns simply as a result of being on the scene and their willingness to take risks.

The oil boom created the need for technical experts. Although no large numbers of Jews became involved, Jewish newcomers with skills filled some of the posts. Louis Loeffler came to Bristow as legal counselor for Bermont Oil and Hughes Drilling Company. Morris Keiser, a geophysicist, moved to Ponca City and served as an exploration expert for Marland Refining and for L. H. Wentz in the mid-twenties. Professional experts of this kind presented a new kind of Jewish presence in small towns where the merchant was the dominant and sometimes the only image of the Jew.

The general development of the state drew other specialized newcomers into some of the small towns. Norman, the seat of the state university, began to receive Jewish faculty members during this period. Nathan Court joined the mathematics department in 1916 and Benjamin Botkin the English faculty in 1921. Fascinated by his new home, Botkin edited a four-volume work of Oklahoman and southwestern folklore and songs entitled *Folk-Say*. The first volume appeared in 1929 and was the first publication under the imprimatur of the University of Oklahoma Press. During the twenties Norman also became the host to a significant number of Jewish students who enrolled at the University. The creation of Jewish fraternities and sororities soon followed.

Despite the slowing down of growth, Jews continued to live in the small towns of Oklahoma during the second and third decades of the century. Their numbers did not increase rapidly and even declined in some places. But new opportunities and new growth in an ever more specialized and developing state economy continued to support and attract them.

The rapid and sustained growth of Oklahoma City and Tulsa between 1907 and 1930 placed the two cities in a separate class as urban centers. Oklahoma City, which appeared as a town overnight with the Run of 1889, achieved its early leadership because four railroads had built into it by 1905. That transportation system made it a trade center able to reach almost every part of the state. Located in the state's geographical heart, the city also developed in the midst of the best agricultural lands, offering diversified crops almost the year round. As a result, a prosperous wholesale and distribution trade grew up on the basis of that agriculture. In 1910 Oklahoma City became the capital of the state, adding to its prestige and drawing people and services into its midst. Only in manufacture did it lag behind its potential.

The solid position of Oklahoma City as a trade center proved attractive for the growth of the Jewish population from its early days. Life there was interesting and promising and newcomers poured in. These came both from outside the state as well as from smaller towns within. The growth of the city supported economic specialization. While Jews earned their livelihood in the familiar mercantile and service occupations that delineated the city's growth, they also played a unique role in defining specialization. The population could now support expensive fashion shops for women, and Jews with experience in large metropolitan areas introduced the styles of the broad outside world to Oklahoma. Al Rosenthal opened a shop under his own name in 1915 after several years in the city and a background of experience in exclusive New York houses. B. J. Kaufman, for a time, operated a wholesale millinery house. In this manner the area of the economy in which Jews were always active deepened, developing more varieties of mercantile enterprise.

The demand for services in a larger metropolis also broadened the range of activity. Ben Barnett, who came to Oklahoma City in 1909, opened a laundry which, in a few years, turned into a chain of businesses. Ben Hirschland, who opened a wholesale paper business before statehood, moved into the manufacture of boxes. By the early twenties his business had grown to include related enterprises as far away as Tulsa and Amarillo. Regional markets became a part of the picture for those who achieved financial success in Oklahoma City.

Furthermore, as the city became an important business and political center, Jews entered the professions in larger numbers, with the law leading the way. Ed Hirsh, long an attorney in Muskogee, came to Oklahoma City in 1920 where he was joined by his son, also an attorney. Max Fagin, who came to Oklahoma City in 1917, became an attorney, and in the late twenties an assistant county attorney. Dr. I. Levy, who had lived in McAlester between 1902 and 1919, opened his optometry practice in Oklahoma City. Dr. J. C.

Fishman joined the University of Oklahoma's School of Medicine in the city.

Tulsa grew at an even more spectacular rate than Oklahoma City between statehood and 1930. Tulsa committed itself early to the development of the oil fields nearby which had been discovered and opened in the first years of the twentieth century. As early as 1911 it was describing itself as "the greatest oil city in the world at the present time."[15] In contrast to Oklahoma City, which took on the characteristics of a regional commercial and political center, Tulsa's commitment to oil contributed to its growth and fame as a national focal point.

The attention Tulsa gained contributed to the growth of its Jewish population. The first Jews who arrived there, apparently around 1902, came from Latvia attracted by the promise of the city. In 1904, when the oil boom had hardly begun, the Simon Jankowsky family moved there from McAlester. By 1918, Tulsa's 500 Jews placed it second to Oklahoma City in Jewish population and it soon passed the capital as the largest center of Jews in the state. While Oklahoma City's Jews had reached 0.86 percent of the population in 1927, Tulsa Jewry had climbed to 1.77 percent of that city's population, probably the highest density in the state.

The pattern of settlement in Tulsa had much in common with that of Oklahoma City. Simon Jankowsky opened Palace Clothiers in 1904 and remained in business until his death in 1943 when his sons took over. Sylvan Goldman, who became one of the most successful businessmen in the state, came to Tulsa in the mid-twenties. His father had made the Run and settled at Ardmore, but the larger city was more suitable for the son's interests and capabilities. Even after he left Tulsa, he settled in Oklahoma City, retaining his metropolitan preference. Tulsa drew Jewish population from within the state and from without like a magnet.

The oil industry could not but leave its special mark on Tulsa's Jews. Specialists came to participate: geologists, engineers, and attorneys with skills in oil and gas law. Oil well supply houses under Jewish ownership appeared. Tax auditors, such as Leo Meyer, a former secretary of state, moved to Tulsa from Oklahoma City. Jews also founded oil companies in Tulsa during these boom years. An offspring of a Jewish oil family, the Aaronsons, recalled the almost chance character of breaking into the industry in the early days. "The *nagid* [rich man] of the present Tulsa community used to be our groceryman. He bought one day, instead of a stock of canned goods, a corner of a corner of an oil field. That was all he needed. By exactly the same kind of purchase my grandfather, who had gone bankrupt in New York, moved to Tulsa and built himself one of the fanciest homes in town. Then he paid off his creditors."[16] This sort of story, like that of the junk dealer with a pipe supply, occurred often in the early history of Tulsa. In addition to the Aaronsons, a number of other names came to the fore among Jewish oil men. Julius Livingston, the Travis brothers, and the Finston brothers were all associated with strong independent firms. Not all of them did equally well but they demonstrated that Jews participated in many branches of Tulsa's major economic activity. They did not, however, enter the top ranks of the major companies.

While the settlement patterns for the two large urban centers were fairly similar, some differences emerged. Tulsa Jewry, unlike the older Oklahoma City settlers, was dominated by more recent eastern European immigrants.[17] That distinction affected internal Jewish organization and attitudes, and also accounted for some greater cultural distance between the Jewish community and its non-Jewish neighbors there than in Oklahoma City. Tulsa's Jews may have prospered more than those of Oklahoma City.[18] Although that conclusion might be explained by the Jewish community's share in Tulsa's marked financial success, the effect on Jewish relations to the rest of the city's population was unclear. In either case, the similarities outweighed the differences and both cities had, by 1930, well-established Jewish populations, largely middle-class, with well-developed roots.

The late twenties were a high point in the history of Jewish population growth and settlement in Oklahoma. In common with the Territory and the state itself, growth had gone on unabated for sixty years with the trend interrupted only by spurts of greater growth. By 1930, however, the condition of the country, the state, and the Jews began to undergo sharp changes. For a quarter century thereafter the Depression, Dust Bowl, Second World War, and altered immigration rules broke the old pattern of growth. Slowdown and even outright decline came to Oklahoma and along with it, to Oklahoma's Jewish population.

Economics alone, however, did not explain the decline among Oklahoma's Jews. New immigration quotas in the mid-twenties reduced the number of Jews coming to the United States. In 1924 nearly 50,000 Jews came to America, a typical figure for the early twenties. Under the new quota, however, it took the next five years combined for that number of Jewish immigrants to come to the country. With the coming of the Depression, even those figures were cut in half, only 26,000 arriving between 1931 and 1937. Even though the rise of Nazism led to an increase in Jewish immigration again, the numbers who entered the country up to the Second World War remained lower than those of the early twenties and much smaller than the yearly contingents arriving in the period prior to World War I.

The effects on Oklahoma were at least partially demonstrable. In 1930, 753 Jews in the state listed Yiddish as their mother tongue; the figure had dropped to 440 by 1940. By 1960 only 177 noted Yiddish as their first language. While data on mother tongues is a limited indicator, it does suggest the drying up of the stream of foreign-born Jewish immigrants into the state. Immigration figures for the state bore out the paucity of new foreign residents. Between 1931 and 1936, the years of the lowest influx, a total of thirty-five Jews selected Oklahoma as their destination upon arrival in the United States. Even in 1939, when immigration began to increase again, only sixty-four Jewish newcomers chose the state as their new home.

The decline of immigration made the question of population growth increasingly dependent on the natural increase of native-born Jews. For a variety of reasons Jews generally produced fewer children than the non-Jewish population. The explanation lay in their heavily urban and middle-class character: city folk generally have fewer offspring than rural folk and native-born Jewish families produced even fewer than their own immigrant predecessors. The higher the percentage of native-born Jews, the smaller the number of children they produced and the greater their urban population, the more the condition affected both their absolute numbers and relative size to the total population.

Nor did the condition of Oklahoma's economy entice any significant domestic migration. The large cities, which were the magnets for Jews through the twenties, continued to grow but at a much slower rate. Oklahoma City, which had doubled in population between 1920 and 1930, rose by only one-third in the next twenty years. Tulsa, which nearly doubled in the twenties, grew by less than 30 percent between 1930 and 1950.

The Jewish population followed patterns established by both urban and state growth. Just as Oklahoma City and Tulsa continued to grow slowly in the thirties while the population of the state as a whole fell, the Jewish population in the two cities also grew while its numbers in the state apparently fell. Oklahoma City had 1,250 Jews in 1927 and 2,100 by 1940. Tulsa, with 2,400 in 1927 counted 2,850 by 1940. Between 1940 and 1954, however, the decline also hit these centers. Oklahoma City's Jewish population fell to 1,750 and Tulsa's to 1,977 in 1954.

The data for the smaller towns were more irregular between 1930 and 1955. In some of the better-known towns the Jewish population declined. Muskogee's numbers went from 200 in 1927 to 155 in 1940 and then to 151 in 1950. Okmulgee, with 125 in 1927, had 100 in 1940, while its absence from tables of towns with 100 or more Jews in 1954 indicated a further drop. Ardmore, however, apparently grew from 67 in 1927 to 110 in 1940 and rose again to 120 in 1954. Some towns appeared to lose their Jewish population entirely between 1927 and 1940.

The Depression years weighed heavily upon the entire population of the state. Per capita income, which stood at two-thirds of the national level in 1929, fell well below that until 1937 after which it began to recover slightly. Only with World War II, when military installations, new industrial facilities, and utilization of resources by nonagricultural areas of the state's economy became significant, did growth resume.

The experience of the Jews in the difficult years of the thirties was varied. In Carnegie, the Grad family, located in the town since 1911, survived the dust and the hardships associated with the period.[19] On the other hand, the May family whose successes from 1910 on had led to the creation of a chain of men's clothing stores in Tulsa, Oklahoma City, Bartlesville, and Muskogee, were hard hit during the dismal period. The Tulsa store, built in the twenties and considered the most modern of its type in the state, did not survive the economic disaster of the early thirties and closed in 1934. One of the brothers, Harry May, moved to San Antonio following its shutdown. The whole chain absorbed the loss but the remaining stores weathered the Depression and recovered well during World War II.[20]

Evidence of financial difficulty appeared in Tulsa. People gave apartment houses away for the payment of taxes owed. A Hebrew Free Loan Association established in 1929 to offer small loans to needy Jews processed only thirteen loans totaling $2,650 in that year. In 1930 the number of loans doubled in the sum of $5,750, while in 1931, thirty-four loans were granted totaling $5,800. In September 1932, Max Kahn, president of the Tulsa Federation of

Jewish Charities, in an appeal for funds, tried to impress the local Jewish community with the seriousness of the economic problem. "Today the depression has changed everything," he wrote. "The Tulsa Federation of Jewish Charities no longer faces the problem of how to help those five hundred or five thousand miles away. . . . In our own city more than twelve families must obtain material support from our charities. . . . We cannot delay their petition with promises of what we will do next month. We cannot send them out to beg. . . . And now our Federation is about to close its doors. No greater catastrophe has ever threatened our Jewish community."[21] While the number of those in need within the Jewish community was small, the suffering was nevertheless real.

Despite the financial difficulties, Oklahoma's Jews, like most other Oklahomans, survived. Even if there was a small population decline, relatively few departed. The drop in immigrant population and relatively low birthrate could as readily account for the decline as any exodus of Jews from the state. By the early thirties so many of Oklahoma's Jews were well established that their departure would not have been easy. And no obvious havens existed to which they could turn for ready solution of their economic problems. The Depression was hardly limited to Oklahoma.

The era of the Second World War was so disruptive of the earlier patterns of settlement that it was exceptional. Military service and the demands of the war effort hampered family life, altered economic activity, and scattered population. The greater part of the decline in the Jewish population for the period between 1930 and 1955 may even have occurred during the war period rather than the Depression.

A general estimate of the immediate postwar years and the early fifties, offered by a leading rabbi in the state, indicated some of the uncertainty of those years. Writing in the mid-fifties, Rabbi Joseph Levenson of Temple B'nai Israel in Oklahoma City spoke of the few Jewish newcomers migrating to the state to establish permanent residence. The children of the pioneers had married, moved, or had been "lost to Judaism through intermarriage and indifference."[22]

The disruption of the war era and the concomitant decline of the Jewish population no doubt weighed heavily on the concerned clergyman. In retrospect the situation may have been less serious than anticipated for the survival of a Jewish community in the state. Even the rabbi admitted that the level of activity in the Jewish community remained high.[23] Moreover, the membership list of Temple

B'nai Israel in 1978 revealed that over one-fourth of the families listed had been present for at least twenty-five years. Considering that death removed many members in that quarter century, the stability, if not the growth, of the congregation may have been greater than it seemed when the judgment was made.

Chapter 3

THE JEWISH COMMUNITY

While Jews came to Oklahoma as individuals seeking livelihoods or joining families, their existence as Jews depended on the creation of institutions which enabled them to identify and maintain themselves as Jews. Jews have been defined both as an ethnic and as a religious group, but their primary identification in Oklahoma has been expressed in religious terms. The chief institution of religious Jews has been the congregation. Composed of Jewish members who formed them when they realized the need to have them and were able to bear the responsibilities, congregations usually were inseparable from the so-called Jewish community. It was their purpose "to care for the religious, educational, charitable, and social needs of the Jews."[1]

The early Jewish settlers, living largely in isolation from each other, could not readily organize congregations, since they lacked the essential requirement of numbers. And while in Judaism the existence of a congregation did not involve the matter of salvation, there were moments in their lives when a communal presence was sorely missed. The celebration of the Sabbath or holiday observance made it important. Certain ceremonies demanded the services of functionaries. Marriage in the faith had to be performed by a rabbi. Ritual purity, particularly with respect to circumcision and the slaughtering of animals for meat involved special training. Some form of association was also necessary for Jews to be buried in accord with Jewish religious custom. In short, Jews who wished to practice traditional customs could not permanently forego all the elements of communal life.

Another condition that complicated Jewish communal life in America was the very openness and inclusiveness of the society. By contrast, until the end of the eighteenth century virtually all

European Jews had lived in communities which served as the agencies of Jewish self-government. That separate existence for Jews arose out of their anomalous position in medieval and early modern European Christian culture. Since the Jews were permitted no real place in the corporate structure of that society, they were granted a separate corporate life outside it. The community's officers were the viceregents for the political rulers in whose territory they lived.

The situation in Europe had required Jews to live together under the laws pertaining to Jews. Within the community this meant living according to its traditional patterns as prescribed by its rabbinical leaders. The synagogue itself was a subordinate institution in which certain communal activities took place, not an independent self-governing body. The rabbis were not employees of the synagogue.

In America no such definition of community existed. The Jewish community was a voluntary one and it possessed no authority to call upon the government for sanctions against recalcitrant members. Congregations could and did form on the basis of varying religious customs, national origins, differences of social class, or purely personal preferences. The desires of the local group were paramount.

Adjustment to America in religious observance depended upon the prior experience of the immigrants as well as their attitudes toward Judaism and their new environment. In general, adaptation came more quickly among those from areas where emancipation had already made inroads or where the pattern of life was closer to that of the United States. The immigrants from central Europe fulfilled these conditions more readily than those from eastern Europe, but all those who came made their own adaptations.

American Reform Judaism paralleled developments in Germany in its origins but took on its own character by the late nineteenth century. Reform Jews characterized their religion as an evolutionary one. Identity, not tradition, was the key. Reform Jews concentrated on the central ethical ideas of the Old Testament rather than the practices of Judaism and often exhibited a strong antiritualistic trend. To those who adopted this view, for example, the dietary laws might no longer be binding. They tended also to reject any Jewish national or ethnic emphasis. To the major spokesman of Reform Judaism, Isaac M. Wise, the watchword "we are Israelites in the Synagogue, and Americans everywhere" summarized the essence of how American Jews should behave.[2] The founding of Hebrew Union College in Cincinnati in 1875 (an important source for rabbis in Oklahoma) marked the coming of age of the Reform movement in America.

Although it was not their monopoly, immigrants from eastern Europe, more accustomed to maintaining the traditional rituals and customs, tended to be classed as Orthodox. The degree of emancipation from the patterns of medieval life had not proceeded as far there as in western Europe. Jews kept their own language for the most part and remained sharply differentiated from the Christian population in legal terms.

The adherents of Orthodoxy, more than other groups among the American Jews, sought to retain control over the education of children and insisted on the use of Hebrew as the language of the Torah. For them, changes had to come through the application of precedent to the new conditions of America. In practice this method of adaptation insured slow change. To uphold their views, in 1896 the Orthodox created their own yeshiva, or seminarial training school, which became the nucleus for the formation of Yeshiva College in 1928.

As the great wave of eastern immigration flowed into the country, the gulf between Reform and Orthodox communities widened. American Jews dissatisfied with the Reformist point of view sought to achieve their own synthesis between the modern United States and Jewish traditional practice. One expression of that search was Conservatism. Its growth came by way of secession from the camp of radical Reform. But the congregations which constituted its membership came largely into the Conservative camp from the ranks of Orthodoxy.[3] The Jewish Theological Seminary, the movement's cornerstone, had been created as early as 1886, but it was not until the early twentieth century that Conservatism received real impetus.

Conservatism did not hold that every word of the Torah and of the Oral Law were literally the Word of God. But unlike the Reformists, who looked only to the moral dimension as binding, the Conservatives held to the Jewish tradition in its entirety "as a steady unfolding of revelation" never wholly free of human limitation or entirely barren of an inspirational spark.[4] In practice, the majority of the Conservative congregations remained close to modern Orthodoxy.

There were too few Jews in the early years of Oklahoma's settlement to permit the establishment of full-fledged Jewish institutions. Nevertheless, they could organize sufficiently to accommodate some of their needs. The mere presence of Jews, however, did not insure the creation of Jewish institutions. Whether or not communal effort took place depended heavily on the desires and determination of the settlers.

The Muskogee experience illustrated this process. Although the Sondheimers were among the earliest Jews in the Territory, this did not automatically guarantee that Muskogee would be the site of the earliest Jewish institutions. For one thing, other Jewish families did not arrive there until almost a generation later, in the middle of the nineties. One commentator noted that the Sondheimer family, while active in Muskogee's civic affairs, "were never particularly concerned with Jewish affairs."[5] Alexander Sondheimer, one of Joseph's sons, married out of the faith in 1895. Although one biographical account written shortly before his death in 1923 indicated his allegiance "to the faith of his fathers," his will left the overwhelming portion of his estate to non-Jewish institutional beneficiaries.[6] Another account indicated that he may have joined the Presbyterian Church.[7] Samuel Sondheimer maintained a closer affinity to Jewish communal affairs, but the Sondheimers did not become fervent initiators of Muskogee's Jewish communal life.

When the second generation of Jewish settlers arrived in Muskogee, group activity increased. In 1905, over a quarter century after the Sondheimers appeared, twelve Jewish families organized Congregation Beth Ahaba. This did not yet mean a full development of Jewish communal activity, since there were insufficient resources to hire a rabbi or build a temple. In those days laymen conducted services in private homes and Mrs. Henry Fist held what may have been the first Jewish Sunday school in Oklahoma in her home. It was not until 1916 that the community invited Edward Israel, a student of Hebrew Union College of Cincinnati, to Muskogee to officiate at the High Holy Day services. He stayed to help the congregation dedicate a temple. In 1917 the community dedicated the first Jewish cemetery in the town.[8]

The Ardmore community showed how numbers and initiative could change the tempo of development. There by 1890, only five years after the first Jews had arrived, the Emeth congregation had been organized by twenty-two families. As in Muskogee, lay leaders conducted services on the Sabbath while rabbinical students from Hebrew Union College were brought in for the High Holy Day services. In 1894 the congregation established a cemetery association and acquired burial ground. In 1903 Sam Daube purchased the old Christian church to serve as a temple and two years later the congregation assumed a formal corporate character. From that time on rabbis from various communities, including Rabbi Blatt from Oklahoma City after 1906, served the congregation occasionally. A knowledgeable layman, Morris Miller, also conducted Friday night religious services fairly regularly, a pattern some communities follow to this day.

The development of Jewish communal institutions in Oklahoma City occurred even more rapidly. The Holy Days were already celebrated there in 1890 with a minyan, the traditional quorum of ten males, composed of local residents and some country peddlers. Although they formed no permanent organizations then, they did charter the Hebrew Cemetery Association of Oklahoma City in 1902, perhaps the first Jewish organization to be incorporated in the state. The growth of the population and the energy of some of those early settlers allowed the creation in 1903 of a congregation still known as Temple B'nai Israel. As in other towns, students from Hebrew Union College were invited to conduct High Holy Day services. The creation of a Sunday school followed shortly thereafter, supervised by correspondence with Hebrew Union College. In 1904 the congregation engaged a rabbinical student, Arthur Lewinsohn. When ill health forced him to give up his duties, he was replaced by Rabbi Joseph Blatt, who came from a congregation in Columbus, Georgia. Rabbi Blatt assumed his duties in 1906 and established a lifelong ministry in Oklahoma City. Thus, by the time of statehood Oklahoma City Jews had taken care of their basic ceremonial needs, the education of the young, and the suitable burial of the dead.

The achievement of a solid and relatively full list of services by the Oklahoma City community provided the impetus to aid Jews elsewhere in the state. Rabbi Blatt, dedicated and able, gave of his expertise in the organization of congregations in Tulsa, Enid, Shawnee, and Ardmore, and performed almost in the manner of a circuit rider for a number of years. As an individual and a rabbi he became a living symbol of the presence of Judaism in the city and to some extent in the state. His voice, even in the early years after his arrival, spoke not only to the Jews but also for them to the Christian community. The growth of one major community thus contributed to the development of others and to the position of the Jews in the general population.

The experience of the Jews in Tulsa in creating a community paralleled that of Oklahoma City. No long delay elapsed between the arrival of the settlers and the first steps of organization. A regular minyan existed as early as 1903. In 1905 the Orthodox families belonging to it brought a *shochet*, a person skilled in the proper methods of ritual slaughter of animals, to their city. In 1912 they purchased land for a cemetery. In 1916, under the leadership of N. C. Livingston, L. E. Z. Aaronson, and Marion Travis, the construction of a synagogue began and was completed a year later. Rabbi Morris Teller became the spiritual leader of that congregation, B'nai Emunah, which exists to this day. In 1916 a religious afternoon school, called a Talmud Torah, was opened. By World War I the major communities of the state had created some of the basic institutions by which Jews measured and preserved their identity.

The establishment of the first formal congregations in Tulsa and Oklahoma City does not adequately illustrate the religious life of those Jews who lived in the many small communities or in isolation. As in the early days of the larger centers, where full organization proved beyond the resources of the local population, partial organization of activities occurred. They brought in rabbinical students for holidays and used rabbis from within the state and even from Texas who visited outlying communities whenever possible. Mostly, those who showed concern for religious life handled their own Sabbath, made private arrangements for the teaching of children or taught themselves. Many associated themselves with the larger city congregations for special occasions if distances were not too great. Often it took considerable effort by all to produce even a minimally satisfactory religious life but the dedicated succeeded in maintaining it sometimes for many years or a lifetime.

While numbers, resources, and motivation influenced the pace of communal organization, they did not account for its cultural variety and complexity. The diverse historical experiences of the Jewish immigrants produced variations of custom among them in their religious practices. Coming from societies that differed widely, Jews adapted and defined themselves according to these environments. When immigration to the United States threw them together their previous experiences carried over, producing tensions among them.

The differences between Reform and Orthodox congregations could be great or relatively minor depending on the attitudes and feelings of the individuals involved. Often the distinctions assumed a social as well as a religious form, and wealth, degree of assimilation, and national origin, came into play. Frequently these distinctions led to the creation of new congregations. In Oklahoma City, where a Reform congregation already existed, the charter for the Orthodox Emanuel Synagogue was obtained in 1904; Orthodox religious services had been held even before that. The importance of Jewish education to those of Orthodox persuasion led them to create a Talmud Torah in 1910. Itinerant teachers who lived with member families helped in this effort and kept expenses low.[9] Fewer in numbers than the Reform group at B'nai Israel, the Orthodox dedicated their synagogue in 1917 and answered for their own spiritual needs until 1921 when the first rabbi joined the congregation.

Unlike Oklahoma City where Reform Jews were the first to organize, the Orthodox Jews led the way in Tulsa. The Reform Jews were not far behind. Rabbi Blatt and A. D. Engelsman, an important communal and civic leader in Oklahoma City, aided and encouraged them. Formal organization meetings of Congregation Temple Israel began at the end of 1914 and in 1917 land was purchased for a suitable structure. In the fall of 1917 Jacob B. Menkes became the rabbi of the Reform congregation. Thus both of the large urban centers had established two of the major formulations of American Jewish practice before the end of the First World War. The four congregations of Tulsa and Oklahoma City have remained the largest and most active in the state.

The continuing changes in American religious life, in time, also affected the major congregations. Orthodoxy in particular faced difficulties of adaptation to American ways and conditions. Where Jews concentrated in heavy numbers, which usually meant centers of recent immigration, it was quite possible to retain traditions. In Oklahoma, however, where at best the Jewish population was diluted by small numbers, scattered living patterns, and the absence of any large-scale influx of new immigrants, the Orthodox believers were hard put to maintain their ways.

The greatest formal changes in Oklahoma began in the 1940s. By then the younger generation of Jews was taking hold. Such customs as separate seating of men and women and the ban on riding to the synagogue on the Sabbath became impossible to maintain. In 1946 Oklahoma City's Emanuel Synagogue joined the ranks of the Conservatives, affiliating with the United Synagogue of America. Rabbi Israel Chodos, who arrived in 1947, followed through with the modernization process.

In Tulsa, B'nai Emunah underwent some of the same kinds of changes. In the forties, under the leadership of Rabbi Norman Shapiro, a graduate of the Conservative Jewish Theological Seminary, the congregation moved briefly into the United Synagogue. His successor, Rabbi Arthur D. Kahn, remained personally committed to Orthodoxy but adopted changes nevertheless. It was only in the seventies, however, that B'nai Emunah formally tied itself to the Conservative United Synagogue. With that step Orthodoxy in its older form disappeared from the scene in Oklahoma.

The differences between the major congregations led at times to strained relations, particularly in the earlier years. As late as 1930 Rabbi Hyman Iola of Tulsa's Temple Israel asked plaintively, "Must the differences between orthodoxy and reform be permitted to crowd out from our vision our common purposes and tasks? Surely Jewish learning ought to prove a common meeting ground...."[10] Rabbi Iola's cry, however, was uttered more in frustration than in despair, for the real despair of the Jews in the twentieth century lay not in their internal tensions but in their treatment by the outside world.

Although differences between the types of congregations remain, the intensity of bad feeling has abated. The common experience in America along with contact in a single community contributed heavily to the softening of mutual attitudes. Succeeding generations in Tulsa underwent an interesting evolution. Not bearing the same burden of distinctions as their parents, younger Jews mixed socially and sometimes intermarried. To bridge family differences or show respect for parents some went so far as to become members in both congregations, Orthodox or Conservative and Reform.[11] Moreover, the enormous problems faced by world Jewry since the 1930s forced unified efforts upon all Jews.

The Census of Religious Bodies, taken decennially from 1906 to 1936, offers a general picture of the religious institutional condition of the Jews of Oklahoma. The census of 1906 reported four congregations in the state. Two of the four reported membership by heads of families, counting twenty-two in Carter County (Ardmore) and fifty in Oklahoma County (Oklahoma City). Two congregations reported having Sunday schools of seven officers and teachers and fifty-two students. By 1916, eleven congregations existed with a combined membership of 1,166. Six of the eleven reported buildings valued at $96,000. Eight commented on their Sunday schools which totaled thirty officers and teachers for 260 students.

At the first peak of Jewish growth in the mid-twenties, the number of congregations actually dropped from eleven to nine. At the same time the number of members rose sharply from 1,166 to 4,098; and while the number of edifices remained constant at six, their value rose to $215,000. Four of the congregations reported Sunday schools of thirty-four officers and teachers and 362 pupils. The data reflected the rising urban concentration of the Jewish population expressed in larger congregations. Interest in Jewish education remained high although the number of children involved may not have kept pace with the growth of the congregations. The slackening birthrate may have been the reason for that since the degree of Jewish affiliation with congregations was quite high.

The next decade, which included the worst years of the Depression, saw the number of congregations actually increase from nine to ten with 5,396 members. Of ten synagogues, six reported a value of $100,250. The Sunday schools of five congregations reported thirty-two officers and teachers for 327 pupils. The incomplete data do not allow a full comparison with the 1926 census, but the report on Sunday schools indicates fewer children enrolled for the still growing congregational membership. As in 1926, the figures for 1936 indicate either declining attendance for religious education or the presence of fewer children. The increasing congregational membership, however, showed continuing religious concern among the parents and a low birthrate primarily affected the decline in religious school enrollment.

Although the temple and synagogue were the focal points of local American Jewish religious life, they did not exhaust the range of Jewish institutional development. Beyond the obligations of prayer, schooling, marriage, and burial, lay the concerns of welfare toward the Jewish community on local, national, and even international levels. The tradition was an old one. Jewish benevolent societies had been founded as early as the eighteenth century in America. German Jews founded B'nai Brith ("Sons of the Covenant") in 1843 to unite all Jews for a variety of purposes including "the wants of the poor and needy; visiting and attending the sick; coming to the rescue of victims of persecution; providing for, protecting and assisting the widow and the orphan on the broadest principles of humanity."[12] In time the philanthropic emphasis of the organization broadened to include educational and political activity. In 1913 it set up the Anti-Defamation League to combat anti-Semitism and in 1923 it established the Hillel Foundation to offer Jewish college students an opportunity to learn about and to participate in Jewish life.

The catastrophic problems facing the Jews of the world gave rise to other American-Jewish organizations. In the early years of the century the American Jewish Committee was formed. The extraordinary suffering caused by the pogrom in Kishinev in 1903 and the Russian Revolution of 1905 led to the organization of campaigns for relief funds and even for Jewish self-defense. The AJC, formally established in 1906, had as its objectives "to prevent the infraction of the civil and religious rights of Jews in any part of the world . . . to secure for Jews equality of economic, social, and educational opportunity; to alleviate the consequences of persecution. . . ."[13] Along with B'nai Brith, the American Jewish Committee became a powerful force in American Jewish life on the national scene, supported actively by many prominent Jews.

Under the umbrella of such institutions, local communities could respond to events and problems involving Jews beyond their own limited range. They could also receive the benefits of whatever advice and support those organizations could offer. Evidence of such activities predated the existence of most congregations in Oklahoma and showed the strong sense of feeling that existed among Jewish settlers for their beleaguered brethren abroad. The campaign for relief of Jewish sufferers of pogroms in the fall of 1905 brought contributions from Ada, Ardmore, Coalgate, Crusher, Hartshorne, Lehigh, Marietta, Muskogee, and Olney, in the Indian Territory; and Anadarko, Blackwell, Cleveland, Enid, Guthrie, Lawton, Mountain View, Oklahoma City, Pawnee, and Prague, in Oklahoma Territory.[14] Even if a few of these contributions came from sympathetic Christians, the widespread response indicated concern and awareness of a larger Jewish unity and the presence in Oklahoma of national institutions to channel the effort.

Another form of reaching out to the wider Jewish world by Jewish Oklahomans was their desire for further knowledge of their own people, history, and faith. Perhaps the first institution they joined beyond the local prayer groups was the Jewish Publication Society, founded in 1888 to publish books of interest to Jews. Oklahoma Jews from Kingfisher and Oklahoma City had joined as early as 1901. By 1908 there were also members in Ardmore and Cleveland, while in 1914 there were fifty-seven members in the state residing in Durant, Marietta, McAlester, and Muskogee, as well as the earlier towns mentioned. Jews looked to the national institutions for support in areas of need which their own local arrangements could not satisfy.

Attachments to the national organizations followed the creation of the congregations. By 1907 Muskogee and Ardmore had linked themselves to B'nai Brith. In 1911 Oklahoma City had its own chapter as did Tulsa in 1914. Later B'nai Brith became one of the major links by which the local Jewish communities in Oklahoma engaged in joint activities on the state level. It still plays an important role in this respect.

Alliance with national associations of Jews also came through the congregations themselves. As early as 1848 Rabbi Isaac M. Wise had called for "an association of Israelitish congregations in North America . . . to defend and maintain our sacred faith. . . ."[15] Wise realized his idea only in 1873, when the Union of American Hebrew Congregations was organized out of Reform groups. The Orthodox groups followed suit forming the Union of Orthodox Jewish Congregations in 1898. The Conservative association, the United Synagogue of America, followed in 1913.

Beyond the inclusion of the local congregations into national associations each congregation also divided itself internally for special purposes. Congregational brotherhoods, sisterhoods, and youth groups, grew up to accommodate philanthropic and social activities. These internal segments of the Jewish community also formed into national organizations. The National Federation of Temple Sisterhoods appeared in 1913 and the Women's Branch of the Union of Orthodox Jewish Congregations in 1920.

Often with less recognition than their male counterparts, Jewish women performed important tasks inside the congregation, in the local community, and even on a national scale. Many women joined the men in running the family business, a common pattern of behavior in the small store. Others formulated and carried through activities that fostered Jewish identity, taught the young, or aided in the realization of social projects within and outside the Jewish community.

Jewish women's groups developed early in Oklahoma, shortly after the formation of the congregations. By 1907 Ardmore had its Hebrew Ladies Aid Society and by 1906 Temple B'nai Israel of Oklahoma City had a sisterhood, whose first president was Mrs. Harry Gerson. In 1913 the latter organization, under the name of Jewish Ladies Aid, had already affiliated with the newly created National Federation of Temple Sisterhoods. By 1916 the Sisterhood Beth Ahaba in Muskogee also had joined the National Federation. Tulsa followed shortly afterwards when the Temple Sisterhood began in 1917 (although a Ladies Aid Society had existed earlier) under the presidency of Mrs. Ed Levin. By 1919 it too had affiliated with the National Federation.

The creation of auxiliary organizations locally soon required cooperation where the work of the organizations created duplication and, at times, misunderstanding. The non-partisan National Council of Jewish Women dedicated to educational and social service had already been formed in 1893. In the 1920s this body stimulated the formation of associations of women's organizations. The national religious associations adopted a similar attitude of cooperation, forming a Conference Committee of National Jewish Women's Organizations in 1925. Local and national cooperation in this manner tended to lessen differences and broaden the efforts of the women.

The desire to foster identity and association within the Jewish community led to attempts to enlarge the sphere of sponsored activities beyond the immediate religious life of the community. At times even the largest communities in the state proved unable to maintain such organizations. Although Oklahoma City's Jews attempted by 1910 to create a Young Men's Hebrew Association (YMHA) as did Tulsa in 1916, following the pattern of its Christian counterpart, neither effort succeeded. Community centers designed to offer facilities to foster ties with Judaism and fellowship among Jews, however, did become realities in both cities.

Tulsa produced a unique expression of broad communal interest with the formation of a Jewish Institute in 1920. The institute acquired its own building and was used for cultural events as well as for meetings of various organizations. It also housed B'nai Emunah's religious school. In the 1920s one could hear both outside lecturers, and lectures in Yiddish and on Yiddish topics by Gershon Fenster, a strong communal leader with decided Zionist inclinations. The institute proved to be a powerful magnet, attracting Jews who were not otherwise affiliated with congregations. It closed its doors in 1930, a victim of the financial difficulties of the times. More typically, congregations in Tulsa and Oklahoma City included space for schools and a wide variety of cultural and leisure activities when they moved into new facilities and as their membership grew.

Other dimensions of Jewish institutional development centered on specific issues affecting Jews, such as the rise of the Zionist movement, the extraordinary dislocation and suffering inflicted upon them during the First World War, or the effects of Nazism before, during, and after World War II. Zionism was a divisive issue among

American Jews in the early decades of the twentieth century. Zionists created small and ineffective organizations in the United States as early as the eighties, but the movement received real impetus only in the late nineties. The Union of Orthodox Jewish Congregations founded in 1898 expressed sympathy for the cause but Reform elements did not on the ground that efforts to establish a Jewish state "do not benefit, but infinitely harm, our Jewish brethren where they are still persecuted, by confirming the assertion of their enemies that the Jews are foreigners. . . ."[16]

The differences between the pro-Zionist and anti-Zionist Jews did not rest only on whether a Jewish state ought to be created. The heart of the matter lay in the issue of the relation of Jewish national feeling and identity with given national environments in which Jews lived. To live in America for the Reform Jews meant to become American, not to risk weakening identity with the host society or to risk creating anti-Semitic feeling within it. In an era when Jewish immigration was high and nativist feelings never far below the surface any taint of divided allegiance could cast doubt on the loyalty of all Jews, not merely the Jewish nationalist.

Not all Reform Jews followed this line. But Rabbi Blatt, a leading figure in Oklahoma for forty years, was strongly anti-national. His position could not but influence sentiment in Oklahoma. His successor, Rabbi Joseph Levenson, recalled that Blatt "staunchly opposed Jewish nationalism and he died broken-hearted (in 1946) in the thought that the Reform movement had made peace with political Zionism."[17]

Despite Rabbi Blatt's position in Oklahoma City and the state, the Zionists did gain adherents among the Jews. A linkage between Oklahoma City and the Federation of American Zionists predated 1915, but it was not strong. Dave Schonwald, a prominent community leader, had formal Zionist ties.[18] In 1930 a Jewish campaign for funds to aid European Jews and to support the creation of a Jewish national home in Palestine led to the formation of an Oklahoma state committee to raise the state's quota of $75,000. While the names of Rabbi Israel Gerstein of Emanuel Synagogue and of other prominent communal leaders of the capital city appeared as backers of the campaign, Rabbi Blatt's name was conspicuous by its absence.

Zionism in Tulsa fared better. Gershon Fenster, who arrived in the city in the early 1920s from Okmulgee, founded the first local chapter in the state of the Zionist Organization of America in 1924. In 1925 it had 150 members. His ties were with the Orthodox B'nai

XTRAORDINARY ANNOUNCEMENT: Jews of Oklahoma –

Dr. Nahum Sokolow
STATESMAN, AUTHOR, PHILOSOPHER, LINGUIST

PRESIDENT OF THE JEWISH AGENCY
FOR PALESTINE

THE OUTSTANDING JEW OF OUR DAY
WILL BE THE GUEST OF

Oklahoma Jewry
DURING THE MONTH OF MARCH

◆●◆

Hon. William Henry Murray
GOVERNOR OF OUR STATE
WILL OFFICIALLY WELCOME OUR
DISTINGUISHED GUEST

A. D. ENGELSMAN, Gen. Chairman   DR. JOSEPH BLATT, Chairman Reception
Committee

State-Wide Reception in Honor of Nahum Sokolow —

— Watch for Further Announcement —

The announcement of a famed Zionist's visit to Oklahoma in 1932. Courtesy of the *Oklahoma Jewish Chronicle*.

Emunah congregation. Julius Livingston, an independent oil man and another member of B'nai Emunah, contributed much to the Zionist movement by becoming president of the Zionist Organization in 1925 and by his participation in campaigns for funds. Efforts to attract young Jewish girls to Zionism led to the formation of Hadassah groups in 1921 under the leadership of Mrs. Emil Salomon and Mrs. Samuel Cheifitz, with special projects to support Palestinian Jewish children and a nurses' training home in Jerusalem. In 1935 Hadassah had 265 members and was the largest organization in the city for Jewish women. As a whole, the Tulsa Jewish community gave Zionism greater emphasis and support than did Oklahoma City. Perhaps the greater strength of Orthodox Judaism in Tulsa and its more diversified Jewish population contributed to this result.

The series of catastrophes that marked Jewish life in Europe after the thirties heightened the concern of American Jews for the safety of their brethren abroad. Even the central agencies of Reform Judaism started to come to terms with Zionism by the late thirties, and World War II hastened the process. The creation of Israel as a Jewish national home in 1948, the goal of the Zionists, ended the debate on whether such a home should exist and placed the question of support in a new context. Few Jews in America asked for a reversal of the historical fact of Israel's existence although questions on the form of support and how to channel it now became the issues of the moment.

The support of Tulsa's Jews for Israel may have reached its peak in 1955. Abba Eban, the Israeli delegate to the United Nations, actually launched a bond campaign for Israel among American Jews in the city on April 15. In one remarkable evening 700 Jewish families in Tulsa pledged $700,000. That performance by Tulsa's Jews demonstrated not only their generosity toward fellow Jews, but also the economic success and the strong solidarity they had achieved as a Jewish community.

The network of organizations dedicated to the support of particular causes and needs, ranging from those of the local congregations to those of the Jews world-wide, eventually became so complex that consolidation was necessary for the sake of efficiency and unity. Covering organizations in the form of "federations" were created to eliminate duplication of administrative cost and effort. Shortly after his arrival in Tulsa in 1930, Rabbi Iola commented on the importance of this solution: "The progressiveness of a city may be judged thus: Has it a Federation?"[19] Tulsa organized a Federation of Jewish Charities in 1920 with representatives of sixteen organizations in the city. Mrs. Emil Salomon became its executive secretary. It handled some cases of local relief each year, the funds coming from member organizations. Itinerant Jews also received temporary aid from the Federation. How well the Tulsa Federation could perform can be seen in 1923, when the Federation, serving 500 Jews, spent $25,000. Dallas, with 8,000 Jews, expended about $8,100, and Wichita, with 300 Jews, expended $500.

Federations devoted to fund raising, of course, could not answer the problems of a fragmented voice on important issues to Jews. To overcome the independent agencies in the name of all, "community councils" developed in the 1930s composed of representatives of all these organizations. Tulsa organized its community council in 1938 and Oklahoma City did so in 1941. These agencies still exist in the seventies.

One sign of the maturity of the larger city communities came at the end of the twenties with the creation of local journals. An

Henry J. Tobias

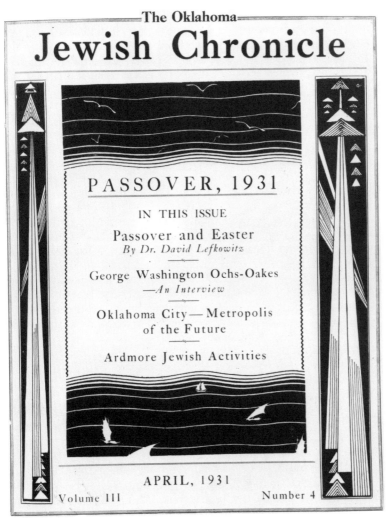

The Oklahoma
Jewish Chronicle

PASSOVER, 1931

IN THIS ISSUE

Passover and Easter
By Dr. David Lefkowitz

George Washington Ochs-Oakes
—An Interview

**Oklahoma City — Metropolis
of the Future**

Ardmore Jewish Activities

APRIL, 1931

Volume III   Number 4

Cover of Jewish journal published in Oklahoma City. Courtesy of the *Oklahoma Jewish Chronicle*.

Oklahoma Jewish Review had appeared monthly in Oklahoma City in 1912. Beginning in 1919 a *Tulsa Jewish Messenger* appeared for a number of years. Neither survived. In 1929 the *Oklahoma Jewish Chronicle* began publication in Oklahoma City under the editorship

45

of Charles I. Cooper. He regarded the publication as a means "to mirror to the community its aims and accomplishments, to serve as a bulletin of its programs, to bring out the latent forces within the group; and to promote cooperation between the communities."[20] The paper underwent minor changes over the years and passed into the hands of Samuel D. Friedman and his wife Mrs. Emma F. Friedman. Under her editorship it continues to appear as a valuable voice for the Jewish community, giving news of social and cultural events, as well as editorials on subjects of importance to all Jews. As an individual effort it is a tribute to the intense dedication of its editors who assumed the burden of its continuing existence.

In Tulsa, the re-creation of a communal publication took place under the auspices of the Tulsa section of the Council of Jewish Women. The first issue of the *Tulsa Jewish Review* appeared in March 1930; like its Oklahoma City counterpart, it continues to exist to the present day. Mrs. Ed Levin and Mrs. Emil Salomon were the driving forces behind its publication in the early years. As a communal rather than an individual project, the Tulsa journal served as the authorized medium for eighteen organizations based in the city, ranging from the Federated Jewish Charities to the Tulsa Zionist Organization and the Jewish National Workers Alliance. Businesslike and efficient, it proved an effective agency for dispensing information and fostering understanding.

The network of institutions created by the Jewish people in Oklahoma was designed to help them practice their faith, support each other in a variety of ways, and maintain their identity. Complex as that network was, even in Tulsa and Oklahoma City, the state's Jews still reflected only a portion of the spectrum of the modern Jewish experience in America. What developed among Oklahoma's Jews compared to what did not helps define the character of the Oklahoma Jewish community.

The nature of Jewish settlement in the state, largely individual in its character, tended to reduce the ethnic component of the community to insignificant proportions. Germanic Jews, who might use their mother tongue among themselves or with non-Jewish German immigrants, had no attachment to the language as Jews but only as Jews who had grown up in Germany. No Jewish institutions devoted to German grew up in Oklahoma.

Yiddish, the mother tongue of the great majority of East European Jews, had a different relationship to Jews. It was transferred to the United States by the East European immigrants after 1880. It had an ethnic Jewish content which many Jews did not readily abandon, because it contained strong emotional commitments. In large Jewish centers a broad cultural life involving Yiddish flourished well into the twentieth century. Every facet of American culture was expressed in Yiddish and the network of institutions using it ranged from newspapers to the theater to a whole school system.

Sizable numbers of Jewish settlers in Oklahoma in the early decades had grown up with Yiddish as their mother tongue. The census of 1910 cited it as the language of 607 of the state's foreign-born residents, at least one-third of the state's Jewish population at that time. Even though interest in Yiddish did surface from time to time, particularly in Tulsa, the emphasis appears almost as a form of nostalgia rather than an effort to maintain and develop a living facet of Jewish culture. No Yiddish-based institutional life grew up and whatever Jewish immigrant settlers brought with them gradually receded into the past. In this sense the ethnic traits of immigrant Jewry fell victim to the strong pull of cultural assimilation.

If cultural assimilation was one characteristic of Oklahoma's Jews, their socio-economic character presented another that distinguished them from Jews in large centers. Middle class in their occupations and goals, they bore no attachment to the radicalism which was an important ingredient of Jewish life in the Russian Empire. A strong Jewish working class and intellectual strain carried over to the United States from Russia. Trade unionism and socialism were live issues among Jews in New York and other large population centers and played a significant role in the development of unions in America, particularly in the garment industry and in socialist political movements. Only the slightest traces of these views appeared in Tulsa where a Jewish National Workers Alliance existed for a time. But it was scarcely a ripple in the Jewish community and attracted little attention or support.

Oklahoma's Jews also adjusted to American culture and to local conditions. Unlike New York, where a segment of businesses catering to the Jewish community followed its traditions closely and kept their businesses closed on Saturdays, most Oklahoma Jewish businesses had to stay open to accommodate their largely non-Jewish clientele. Only on the High Holy Days could they afford to follow their religious inclinations.

Adjustments appeared also in the old traditions. The Reverend Aaron Hardin of Emanuel Synagogue in Oklahoma City arrived in 1946. He taught at its Hebrew school for over twenty-five years.

Although quite traditional, he prepared girls for Bat Mitzvah, the rite of formal entrance into the adult community long restricted to males, and even taught them to read the Torah. In part, Reverend Hardin's decision reflected his personal liberal viewpoint, in part, his desire to reach as many students as he could.[21]

A fairly large proportion of Oklahoma's Jews affiliated with congregations. This was probably a greater share than did so in the areas of largest Jewish concentration in the country. This record reflects both the greater homogeneity of the smaller communities and the greater isolation of the Jews as a small minority. Those who had any desire to maintain their Jewish identity tended to formalize it —both for their own and their children's sakes. In some respects the high level of adherence to congregations also reflects the general culture of Oklahoma and its region, where church attendance and religion have traditionally been important. For those seeking to assimilate in a cultural sense, affiliation could prove an easy adjustment.

The cohesion of the Jewish community in Oklahoma rested not only on faith and institutions, but also on the ties of kinship. Even a cursory glance at the family trees of older Oklahoma Jewish families reveals the marriage ties, the branching out of the siblings of a single generation into separate towns, and children in one town and parents in another. Those ties keep many of Oklahoma's Jews in touch with one another and aware of a dimension of relationship which is powerful and long lasting.

Despite difficult adjustments to the local environment and differences from Jewish communities elsewhere, Oklahoma's Jews created a well-established Jewish life. The religious element of Jewish life held priority over other elements, although the awareness of the condition and needs of Jews elsewhere remained important. Denominational differences, although mildly troublesome at times, did not split the community. Personal differences within congregations may have been sharper. The efforts of Oklahoma's Jews to maintain a Jewish presence has, within their capabilities, proven a successful enterprise.

Chapter 4
THE JEW AND GENTILE INTERACT

How the Jewish and non-Jewish populations acted toward each other was an important dimension of the Jewish experience in Oklahoma. The Jews who came to Oklahoma realized they were entering an area where few Jews lived. To their faith in their ability to succeed economically they added the belief that they could adjust to a new environment and be accepted openly as good citizens and full and equal members of the community. The burden of Jewish history offered no assurances that faith in the tolerance of neighbors was well-grounded.

Arriving alone or joining family members or friends already here, these early settlers had to consider seriously their relationship to the vast majority who were Christian. Usually isolated from other Jews, their economic and perhaps even their personal welfare depended on their capacity to live with the Christian population on a basis of trust and cooperation. To gain that trust they needed to reach out in a manner comprehensible to the gentiles, to work with them, and to participate in the general life of the community. It was reasonable to assume that the greater the degree of their isolation from the Christian population the smaller their chances of success.

They had to face the difficult question of how to maintain their Jewish identity and still become a part of the larger community. The form and degree of Jewishness maintained by the early settlers stemmed from attitudes that pre-dated their experience in Oklahoma. Their new environment, however, could cause them to modify their views. To meet and live closely with non-Jews, given their isolation, could impose conditions in which strict observance of traditional customs became difficult. The demands of business often required keeping stores open on Saturday, the Jewish Sabbath. Dietary laws might prove impossible to maintain. Clearly, those Jews who would insist on the most literal observance could not readily tolerate such departures from practice. The most likely settler was one who accepted a large measure of cultural assimilation and the willingness to tolerate less than the most rigorous schedule of practices known to Jews.

The earliest Jewish pioneers, who were mainly central European Jews, usually adhered to Reform Judaism or were only minimally concerned with religious affairs. Religion often belonged to the private world of the home or temple. In America they behaved as Americans of the Jewish faith, differing from natives only in language skills, a problem experienced by all non-English speaking immigrants. They were perhaps best suited of all Jewish immigrants to deal with the conditions of the frontier and they became the most successful of the early Jewish settlers.

In the first decades of settlement direct personal relationships were the most important element in business survival and general community development. Few formal institutions of a business or social nature existed, and there was little or no Jewish community upon which to rely. Cooperation was a necessity for all.

Examples of and testimonials to the outgoing character of the Jewish settlers are legion. Participation was the keynote. As early as 1880, Joseph Sondheimer offered prizes for quality hides at a fair in Muskogee and in the last years of the century Jake Bodovitz of Ardmore organized merchants to fight unjust taxes in the Indian Territory.[1] Decades later one pioneer recalled the Sondheimers as "[having] had a great deal to do with the building of Muskogee" and as persons who "were always in the forefront when any movement for the upbuilding of the city was proposed."[2]

How far the early Jews could reach out into the community can be seen in the will of Alexander Sondheimer who was killed together with his wife in an automobile crash in 1923. Sondheimer left the largest bequests to the YMCA and YWCA ($150,000 each), while the Boy Scouts received $50,000 and the United Charities a like sum. In addition, he left $50,000 to the First Presbyterian Church and the same amount to Temple Beth Ahaba. Clearly, the general service and charitable organizations of the community occupied a strong place in Sondheimer's attentions in Muskogee.

As Oklahoma's towns grew they began to acquire new economic and social institutions to accommodate new needs and aspirations. In this respect they developed as did urban life elsewhere in the country. The *Standard Blue Book of Oklahoma* of 1910–1911 re-

I wish to thank my many Jewish friends for their support in the Democratic Primary July 29, when I received the greatest number of votes of any of the five candidates.

On August 12, you will again have the opportunity of voting for me, and I sincerely trust that you will investigate my past record sufficiently to assure you that my election will mean a new deal at the Court House and an honest and fair administration of the county government.

FRANK McCALL

Candidate for County Commissioner, Third District

CAPABLE   COURTEOUS   EFFICIENT

Bert McDonel

DEMOCRAT FOR

STATE AUDITOR

SHOULD WIN—HE IS THE ONLY AUDITOR IN THE RACE

Yes, BERT McDONEL is in the run-off primary and can win! PUT A NEW MAN IN THE STATE CAPITOL—A MAN WHO HAS THE COURAGE TO FIGHT FOR YOUR BEST INTEREST.

WM. H. (Alfalfa Bill) MURRAY said in a recent address that Frank C. Carter (my opponent) was a "corporation Flunkie." This can never be said about BERT McDONEL. He has financed his own campaign and can serve all tax payers alike.

BERT McDONEL, is the only ex-service man in this race (served two years overseas). He served his country in time of need, now give him a chance to serve as STATE AUDITOR. He "deserves" your support.

The Voice of the People.....

Not only in the ancient Hebrew (Kol Amon Kekol Shaddai), but in all the tongues of the old civilizations was it accepted as axiomatic, that the voice of the people is the voice of God.

How else can you explain the remarkable outpouring of enthusiastic support to that plain man from Tishomingo?

Oklahoma pioneer, risen from the ranks, not unlike Jefferson, and Jackson, and Lincoln,—

With a mission to set our House in order; to give emphasis to the needs of the masses—

Remember this, you merchants and middle men and manufacturers and producers.

You can have prosperity only to the extent that the farmers and workers have prosperity.

The readers of the Oklahoma Jewish Chronicle come from a people that has at all times stood for social justice.

WILLIAM HENRY MURRAY

Let Us Make It Unanimous!

Vote for Wm. H. Murray for Governor

Election appeals to Jewish voters, 1930. Courtesy of the *Oklahoma Jewish Chronicle.*

vealed that the towns already had spawned an impressive crop of chambers of commerce, Elks lodges, Rotary clubs, and a wide variety of cultural organizations and social listings.

Jews participated quite actively in this early stage of institution building. By 1910 Seymour C. Heyman of Oklahoma City was a Past Exalted Ruler of the Elks Lodge which had been formed in 1898 and Rabbi Blatt had been its chaplain. Heyman was active in the Men's Dinner Club, a director of the Fair Association, and a member of the Oklahoma Art League. Mrs. Solomon Barth worked with the Ladies Music Club. The list of Jewish families noted in the social directory of the city was lengthy. This indicated how much the Jews of the city partook of these general secular social, economic, and cultural activities and the extent to which they were accepted as members of the community.

Smaller towns also offer ample evidence of strong Jewish participation in the building of social and economic institutions. The May family opened a clothing store in Bartlesville in 1910. Jake May, who managed the store after his release from military service in the First World War, was a charter member of Kiwanis and its president for two terms. He also served as president of the Bartlesville Chamber of Commerce and was a member of the YMCA board of directors for twenty-five years. He was also a charter member of the American Legion. Civic minded Jews in Muskogee, Lawton, Ardmore, and Blackwell, matched the range and pattern of his participation.

In Tulsa Jews helped create a civic institutional life. They were among the founders of the Rotary and the Lions clubs and active in the Chamber of Commerce, the Junior Chamber of Commerce and the YMCA. But there is some evidence that in Tulsa Jews encountered a degree of resistance in their efforts to take part in the public life of the community.

The open social mixing which characterized the approach of the Jews to the general community and their acceptance may have reached its peak prior to World War I. By then many of the major institutions of urban economic and social development had appeared. The postwar period witnessed further growth but attitudes underwent some change. Suspicion of Jews and foreigners together with the quest for status altered the relative freedom and ease of mingling that had existed earlier.

Some of these characteristics showed up in Tulsa which had grown rapidly in size and wealth. In some respects the developments there appeared to imitate the genteel anti-Semitism of older Eastern areas. In interviews conducted in the forties, Randall Falk encountered evidence of the change. The Tulsa City Club, founded in 1925, had two Jews among its charter members and another joined shortly after its formation. Falk's evidence indicates that the Club "quickly closed its membership to further Jewish applications." Moreover, he notes, "The discrimination policy finally became so obvious that the three Jewish members resigned."[3] Other interviews reveal restrictions in Rotary and the Lions although these cases appear less flagrant.

Although few persons may have been directly affected, perhaps the most galling rebuff experienced by the metropolitan Jews came at the top of the socio-economic ladder—in the country clubs. The pattern of total or near-total exclusion that existed in many parts of the country was emulated in Tulsa and to a somewhat lesser extent in Oklahoma City. Maurice Sanditen, even as president of the Tulsa Chamber of Commerce, experienced rejection to membership. These instances of intolerance rankled and saddened the Jews who saw them as slights to people who had gone far to contribute to the welfare of the local community. In recent years this condition has softened to some degree.

While Jews contributed heavily to the business and social development of the towns in which they lived, their role in the cultural development of the state was even more marked. Whether in the arts or in education their participation was ubiquitous. The impetus for their ardor had many sources. But their strong faith in education as a means of improvement for the individual and society, and their experience as products of differing cultures probably accounted for their desire to create a broad cultural life in Oklahoma.

The contribution of Oklahoma's Jews in support of culture might well be studied by itself. It extended from the work of Seymour Heyman, who served as president of the Board of Education in the early twenties, to the creation of endowed chairs at the University of Oklahoma and Oklahoma City University by Sylvan Goldman. Heyman, who, according to one historian, deserved a monument for his work, also labored in the Oklahoma Art League as early as 1911 for the creation of an art museum for the city.[4] Numerous others concentrated on seeking to increase the role of music in the city.

In Tulsa, where wealth concentrated more rapidly and where the influence of national standards may have been stronger, the efforts of Jews to improve the cultural life of the city were even greater than in Oklahoma City. Simon Jankowsky was one of the original patrons of what has been called "the first cultural venture" in the city, the presentation of the Chicago Civic Opera.[5] Gershon Fenster, a stalwart of the Jewish community, served as the director of the Philbrook Art Museum. A collector himself, Fenster was honored by the creation of a Jewish museum in his name after his death. In recent years David Milsten has served as director of the Gilcrease Museum; he is also past president of the Tulsa Opera Association. The efforts of Alfred Aaronson may well have been responsible for the retention of the Gilcrease collection in the city. These contributions of Jewish citizens to Tulsa are only some of the more obvious and well-recognized examples of their efforts.

The role of the Jews in philanthropy has not lagged behind their efforts in other fields of public endeavor. In part, the Jewish institutional network has been used to further philanthropic ends but individuals have also participated heavily. As in the case of the arts, a systematic survey could well occupy a separate study. All in all, the efforts of the Jews to participate in the community for its enrichment from the early years to the present have been remarkable for the size of the community. Their labors indicate a desire for acceptance as good citizens of the state and all Oklahomans have gained from this initiative.

The interaction of the Jew and Christian in Oklahoma, by definition, involved not only how Jews behaved toward the general community but also how that community behaved toward them. The relationships of the Christian to the Jew were as old as Christianity itself. The diversity of attitudes about Jews could include a broad spectrum of the feelings which any group of people can hold toward any other. Moreover, they were subject to change under the circumstances of time and place. Just as Jews who migrated to Oklahoma carried their culture with them, so too did the Christians. The nature of that culture, insofar as it concerned the Jews, was a complex mixture of Christian views and American secular beliefs. Like the Jews, the Christians would also be affected by the specific environment in which they lived.

American Christians viewed the Jew in varied ways in the early twentieth century. He was regarded as an immigrant, an alien of a special religious type, and as a person with a unique connection with finance. Jews were also seen in a more neutral but nonetheless disturbing light of a mysterious figure, somewhat removed from the general population.[6] Jews could also be viewed through the open character of American society based on individual merit and democracy. The beliefs and feelings of American Christians, however, also had to stand the test of personal relationships, the fact of Jews living in their midst.

The composite effect of these sometimes contradictory factors produced a dichotomy. The small size of the Jewish population and its urban character did not readily allow persons from rural and interior areas of the country to meet or know Jews. At times that permitted the commonly held negative stereotypes to hold sway over their feelings. The 1920s were a time, for instance, when anti-Jewish feelings were quite strong, particularly in rural and small town areas. However, even then Christians did not necessarily apply the logic of their negative stereotypes against the few Jews who lived among them; local Jews were accepted despite these beliefs.[7]

The sense of mystery and uncertainty about the Jews also was a powerful current. Even Oklahomans well-disposed toward American liberal principles and filled with good will sometimes could not fathom the Jews. The *Tulsa Daily World*, commenting on the rise of anti-Semitic feeling in the country, queried in 1922, "Why is it that Israel remains today in all things peculiar to itself the same as in the days of Moses?" And equally important, the paper continued, "Why is it that despite the lack of political ambition of Israel it sooner or later arouses in every race an aversion and a jealousy that not only invites but precipitates programs [pogroms] and occasions opposition against the Jew?" Admitting that the Jews had played "a wonderfully important and constructive part in the development of a continent," the *World* nevertheless located the source of hatred in "the ancient quality of Israel — its inability or refusal to merge or assimilate." The Jew was "exclusive in his social relations. He associates with Jews and he marries Jews and breeds Jews." This "peculiarity" might be due to the attitude of gentiles, the paper admitted. But it remained mystified, acknowledging that here in the land of equality and freedom the history of the ages was repeating itself.[8]

The editorial revealed a good deal about attitudes. Seeking to be just, the *World* condemned unfairness in the name of the principle of equality before the law. It admired the dedication and the initiative of the Jewish population. Its own Christian and assimilationist thrust, however, would not allow it to accept the differences without at least implying that those who differed were somehow mysterious and perhaps to blame if they suffered for being different. Given the *World's* uneasy benevolence, those less inclined toward good will could readily proceed on a more hostile line.

The early history of Oklahoma reflected some of the traditional signs of American Christian culture. A draft of the state constitution in 1906 referred in the preamble and body to Jesus and to matter capable of being interpreted as a basis for religious legislation. Some "Hebrew citizens of Enid" and other unspecified persons from Vinita petitioned the constitutional convention to eliminate these passages.[9] The petitioners succeeded in their purpose and the *American Jewish Year Book* reported with satisfaction that "the protest of the Jews against the recognition of Jesus in the new constitution of Oklahoma had its effect."[10] The attempt to include such terminology, of course, indicated some lack of sensitivity toward the Jewish population as well as a disregard for the separation of church and state. But it also showed that Oklahoma's Jews felt certain enough of their position to stand up for their rights and that Oklahomans recognized the validity of their complaints.

A few years later a far more painful event stirred the open protest of Jewish leaders in the state. The location of the state's capital aroused a heated controversy between partisans in Guthrie, the temporary site of the capital, and those favoring Oklahoma City, which finally gained that political plum in 1910. A court test followed. The Guthrie *Daily Leader* sought leverage to reverse the course of events. In the process it lashed out in unmistakably anti-Semitic fashion to discredit Oklahoma City. "Shylocks of Oklahoma City Have State By the Throat," read a banner headline on November 1, 1912. The paper detected an "Unparalleled Conspiracy of [sic] the Part of Jews and Gentiles of a Rotten Town to Loot the State for Twenty-five Years."[11] Stressing the role of Jewish landlords and resorting to parodied Yiddish accents to describe the dialogue of the miscreants, the *Leader* hoped to destroy Oklahoma City's hold by revealing a dishonest plot.

Rabbi Joseph Blatt defended the outraged honor of the Jews. In a letter to voters he labeled the alleged plot a lie, defended the persons named, and excoriated the *Leader's* attempt to create prejudice against the Jews. The charges, he wrote, were "a disgrace to the civilization of our state." If this use of prejudice succeeded, he warned, it would become a regular tool. Rabbi Blatt appealed for support against the Guthrie paper "and others of its ilk" to demonstrate the folly of arousing religious prejudice.[12]

THE GUTHRIE DAILY LEADER.

VOLUME XXXIX   GUTHRIE, OKLAHOMA, FRIDAY, NOVEMBER 1   PRICE 5c

SHYLOCKS OF OKLAHOMA CITY
HAVE STATE BY THE THROAT

Levy Brothers, Jewish Landlords, Contribute Ten Thousand Dollars To The Capital Campaign

SECRET CONTRACT MADE THAT THEIR RENT ALL WILL BE RE CUT OFF WHICH MEANS NO STATE HOUSE SHOULD YES VOTE LOSE NOV 5

Desperation: Conspiracy on the Part of Jews and Gentiles of a Rotten Town to Loot the State for Twenty Five Years. An Appalling Story of Chicane, Dishonesty and Corruption.

Special to the Daily Leader.

Oklahoma City, Oct 31. Jerusalem. The cat is out of the bag.

The truth is all its appalling nakedness is known. "Where does Oklahoma City's campaign fund come from?" was the question asked three weeks ago by politicians over the state.

There was no answer then.

In answer now—

Oklahoma City it is the hands of the Shylocks.

The State of Oklahoma will also be in their hands if the proposed amendment to the constitution to locate the capital at Oklahoma is defeated at the polls on next Tuesday.

Intensity at the mercy of greed of financiers will Oklahoma be if after Nov 5 by artifice, misrepresentation, bulldozing and chicanery Oklahoma City succeeds in deceiving the electorate of the state.

"But where did and do the funds come from?" is asked.

Answered now.

From the Levy brothers, of Texas and Oklahoma City. On Aug 31, the Levy brothers subscribed $5,000 to the Oklahoma City capital campaign fund. On Sept 1 the Levy brothers subscribed another $5,000. On Sept 30th, the Levy brothers subscribed a third $5,000, and on Oct 18th, the Levy brothers put up $5,000 more making an aggregate of $20,000.

Who are these Levy brothers? is asked.

Quickly answered. The Levy brothers are the moneyed creditors of the State of Oklahoma. They are the landlords of Oklahoma.

In brief, the Levy brothers are the owners of the buildings where tax capital offices are now located.

When Oklahoma City is the campaign of 1910 prove and free rein to the State of Oklahoma for the capital and after danger and fuss Hastings finally acknowledged that it did not know when it said where it offered free rent to the ... it was the tone public politics many Levy brothers houses and building owners, who jumped upt the offing and agreed to house the capital offices.

It has been a great inducement for the Levy brothers. They have been paid close to almost $61,000 in rentals. For the Levy brothers has been so good, in fact, that they are unable to see the capital moved from Oklahoma City.

The Levy brothers came to Oklahoma City from Texas five years ago. They care nothing about Oklahoma in addition. All they want is "deal s" and more. They are getting it.

Now suppose any Levy brothers have their interest and that of the Oklahoma City capital fund?

Let it not be understood that the brothers Levy are unfair to it. They did not graciously pay over the trust. Their general, the graven were exceedingly well and long than they pay.

And thereby hangs a tale of depredation conspiracy against it by Jew's industry. What is the story? THE LEVY BROTHERS HOLD A SECRET CONTRACT FOR THE STATE CAPITAL OFFICE ...

of Levy brothers becomes public and will be duly placed on file. They will have full sway for eleven years, and will reap revenue aggregating in that time $484,000.

Can the Levy brothers afford to put up $20,000. Well, rather. Of course, if the an vote from the Jews are not $30,000, but some God! Dink out to us. If we do win? If required coaxing, in fact, browbeating on the part of the Oklahoma City capital committee to force the Levy brothers to see the light and come through, but they finally came and hence Oklahoma City has sufficient funds to use expeditiously in the closing days of the campaign and at the polls. Of course no thought was taken of the $484,000 to be borne by taxpayers.

What is the purpose of such a lease? is asked.

The discerning will quickly perceive—

IN THE EVENT OKLAHOMA CITY RETAINS THE CAPITAL ELEVEN (11) YEARS ARE TO ELAPSE BEFORE A NEW STATE HOUSE IS BUILT AND FINISHED

For eleven years the taxpayers must pay rents aggregating $53,000 yearly, not only to the Levys, but to the Lawrences, the Osbrecks, the Larrimores and the others.

What does this mean It means taxes must be raised to pay $483,000 for eleven years of rental. This in the face of Oklahoma City's offer of "rents absolutely free to the state."

The conspiracy is too appalling to sanely contemplate.

The question is asked.

What right has Oklahoma City or its committee to enter into a secret lease for eleven years?

No right at all, but in this case, as in the bond deals, in the $100,000 warrant deals, and the school board loot, Oklahoma City and its committee assume the right. Oklahoma City is strong on the assumption of right.

The conspiracy came to light inadvertently last night, when a copy of the secret lease was sent to a local attorney for approval as to legal verbiage.

Trenchant representations were made to the Jew landlords that they were safe; that the legislature could be handled "gracefully" to Oklahoma City and that while a $1,900,000 appropriation would be put through that no steps would be taken to build a state house. The lays and more delays, it was argued to the Levys, would consume eleven years and Jerusalem! look at the West.

So a written the rankest chapter of look known in the West.

"YES"

VOTE OF REASON ON NO. 40

If by your vote the State Question No. 40 is defeated and the state capital is retained in Oklahoma City, you thereby instruct your representatives in the legislature to go to Oklahoma City in January and cast his vote for state taxes on you.

If you vote "No" you approve of Oklahoma City's course in failing to pay the expenses of moving the capital from Guthrie to ... You also approve Oklahoma City's course in failing to give the rentals, and in charging $53,000 to house state offices.

If you vote "yes" you instruct your legislator to vote for a uniform dollar appropriation for a new statehouse which will not be erected for eleven years, the state is the meantime paying $53,000 yearly in rentals.

In short, if not vote "No" it allow Oklahoma City to saddle an enormous ... defraudance on the state.

If you vote "Yes", the brothers Levy find Oklahoma City has failed to make good, that they must live there, lose... but more importantly, bide state offi...

BIG DRAG IS OFF IN SOUTHWEST

FARMERS WILL VOTE "YES" ON CAPITAL QUESTION DON'T CARE TO VISIT

CAPITAL TITLE PERFECT

Transfer of Capital Park to City Passed On By The Two Courts

VOTE ON CAPITAL

These two instances were the most prominent affecting the Jews of the state before the First World War. If the first reflected ignorance or lack of concern for the presence of a Jewish population, the second showed a clear desire to exploit the feelings assumed to be present for political purposes. However unsuccessful, the attempt demonstrated that there were people in the state prepared to tie stereotypes of the Jew as a crooked operator, a Shylock, to practical political questions. The affair distressed Oklahoma's Jews although it failed to achieve what the *Leader* hoped and quickly faded from the news.

More serious and potentially more dangerous were the changes introduced by World War I and the years following its conclusion. The American entry into the conflagration in 1917 aroused patriotic passions and suspicion of anything deemed foreign. Some of these feelings persisted into the postwar years. In Oklahoma, with its heavily native-born population, feelings toward the foreign-born or those with foreign sounding names were strong. Jews occasionally felt the pressure generated by those feelings.

Shortly after the war, the Madansky brothers found themselves in this situation. Ben Madansky, who had gone to Mexico with a chamber of commerce group from Oklahoma City to investigate an investment opportunity, was embarrassed by having to prove his citizenship upon re-entry into the country. That incident, along with the condition described above, convinced him and his brothers that they had to "Americanize" their surname. On March 9, 1921, the family changed their name to May. To explain the change to the public, the Mays took out advertisements in *The Daily Oklahoman* of Oklahoma City and in local papers where they had stores.[13] The advertisements explained their position. "For many years," one of them read, "we have suffered embarrassment in bearing a distinctly Russian surname and for the past four years our surname has often caused us, not only embarrassment but even annoyance. Since we are all Americans and rearing our families as such, and, since we resent any imputation reflecting upon our Americanism, we have . . . contemplated changing our surname so that we may become even more American . . . and leave no handicap . . . to our posterity."[14] Although the family acted without compulsion and took pride in their act, the affair reflected clearly the pressure that could operate against those deemed suspect by virtue of foreign birth.

Private reactions to the decision of the May family reflect some ambivalence about their decision. One friend, a Bartlesville attorney,

Madansky Brothers Americanize their name

To be known hereafter as May Brothers

WITH this announcement we take the final step to prove ourselves wholly American in every sense of the word. We have eliminated those parts of the name Madansky that are of foreign origin. We wish to forever renounce the name that reminds us of our foreign birth. From this date forward the individual members of this firm and their families will be known as May. Our stores in Oklahoma City, Tulsa and Bartlesville will be conducted under the name of May Brothers.

THIS may seem a radical step to those who know us personally and know of the Good Will and confidence we have built up for our former name. Some have counseled us against this action because of the respect in which the name Madansky is held wherever it is known. They have spoken of the many thousands of dollars we have spent to advertise our ideals, our principles and our methods, in the upbuilding of our businesses.

YET were it inevitable that we give up all the success that has come to us and again build our business from the very beginning, we would not hesitate to take the step we have decided upon. We do not believe such a course will be necessary. We believe that true Americans everywhere will accord us their full sympathy and will approve of our decision.

THERE has never been a time since we first came to the United States---more than thirty years ago---that we have not been Americans in heart and deed. We have appreciated possibly more than can you who never suffered under the heel of Russian Autocracy, the great privilege of being American citizens. We are daily thankful for the Liberty, Opportunity and Happiness that all may have in this land of Freedom.

NEED we add that there will be no change in our policies or methods. Nor will there be any change in the personnel of the firm. We will endeavor to merit an even greater degree of public confidence in and respect for the name May Brothers, upon those same principles that have brought us such a great measure of Good Will; principles that have in fact made this the largest clothing business in Oklahoma.

May Brothers

The Madansky brothers change their name. Courtesy of the *Daily Oklahoman*, March 27, 1921.

wrote, "If all the May brothers . . . are of the good stuff as the one or two I have the pleasure of knowing, it would make no difference to me about how many letters were in the surname, place of birth, religion, or anything else."[15] A Chicago supplier to the firm mused, "it seems almost a shame to discontinue the use of the name you have established so thoroughly throughout Oklahoma."[16] However, another supplier from Fort Worth applauded the action, saying, "we appreciate the courage and good judgment displayed in making your name short and thoroughly American."[17] All wished the family well and praised the step in the last analysis. But some comments indicated that despite recognition of the strong nativist feeling that induced the step, there were those who preferred less accommodation.

The most dangerous and disturbing appearance of the twenties, in Oklahoma, however, sparked in part by the nativist impulse, was the rise of the Ku Klux Klan. Unlike the low-level general hostility toward Jews which formed one element of American Christian culture, the Klan specifically and boldly singled out Jews as one of the anathematic groups of the population. The Jews were not, of course, the sole or even the major target of the Klansmen. They also included aliens, Catholics, radicals, and blacks on their list of undesirables. The directness of the Klan's attack, its methods of operation as a secret and violent organization and its temporary success as a movement distinguished it as a greater threat to the Jews in Oklahoma than anything they had faced up to that time. Moreover, the Klan in Oklahoma was more violent than in any other state in the twenties.[18]

White, Protestant, and nativist in its loyalties and membership, the Klan attacked the Jews at many points. Among the grounds were that they did not worship in Protestant churches, that they were despoilers of the population, and that their influence on cultural life was corrupt. The Klan attacked both Jewish and Catholic businesses, sometimes in favor of Klan business under the acronym TWAK, Trade With A Klansman.[19] Jews were rarely the victims of direct attack, but the Klan thrived as much on threat as on actual force. Economic boycotts hurt even without physical violence. The Jewish population felt weak and relatively helpless because of its small size and distinctiveness.

The threat of the Klan declined after the mid-twenties and with it some of the more overt and cruder aspects of anti-Semitism. Anti-Semitism, however, was more widespread than before the war. The fear of radicalism, stirred by the Russian Revolution, added heat and the image of the Jew as radical, however inappropriate in Oklahoma, took root. The myth of a Jewish international conspiracy to take over the world became an important element in anti-Jewish thought.

New dark clouds on the Jewish horizon gave further strength to anti-Semitism in the thirties. The Depression brought forth its share of economic discrimination while the rise of Nazism in Germany gave impetus to a host of new movements in the United States. In 1934 such organizations as the Silver Shirts, strongly anti-Jewish in their ideology, appeared in Oklahoma. William Murray, the governor and longtime political figure in the state, denounced them. The Tulsa Jewish community sought to alert all to their pernicious effects. A group led by D. R. Travis sought the support of William Skelly, one of the most prominent of Oklahoma's oil men, to prevent them from establishing a headquarters in Tulsa and apparently succeeded.

A few years later, as war again enveloped Europe, and the question of American participation arose, Jews were criticized by a segment of the population as interventionists. The same William Murray, now failing politically, began to attack Jews even though earlier in his career he had found them to be valuable citizens and had actively sought their support. By 1940 Murray linked Communists and Jews and associated his name with such anti-Semitic extremists as Gerald B. Winrod. In the opinion of his biographer, Murray became "a racist of unbounded hatred."[20] Murray's anti-Semitism came at a time when his political and personal powers were on the decline, but the fact that he had been a major political figure in the state made his views saddening to Oklahoma's Jews.

The taint of racism and anti-Semitism did not easily wash off. Tulsa in particular gained something of a national reputation as a center for radical right movements. Those movements and persons, however, often had only nominal attachment to the city. They apparently had less importance for resident Jews than for the image of the city nationally. Nevertheless, some felt that a perceptible withdrawal from active political participation by Tulsa's Jews resulted from its reactionary political climate.

More subtle expressions of prejudice also existed—as they did in the whole society. Part of the reason for the creation of Jewish fraternities and sororities on campuses was to offset the exclusionary social policies which Jewish college students encountered. Life became too difficult at times for some young Jewish Oklahomans and in the twenties they transferred to out-of-state institutions to escape rejection and loneliness. Even when persons lived peaceably and without fear of physical harm among their neighbors they experienced the slurs and vocabulary that revealed hostility toward Jews generally if not toward them personally. In short, the legacy of the centuries of hostility existed in the state despite the spirit of good will and cooperation which characterized the West at its best.

Alongside the anti-Semitism and lesser forms of prejudice, Jews also found generous and tolerant feelings, trust, cooperation, and sympathy toward them as human beings and as Jews. Time and again infant Jewish congregations found temporary quarters in local churches before they had established their own, or a supply of Old Testaments from Christian friends to aid them in their educational programs. More dramatic evidence of good will appeared in hard times. In April 1970, when B'nai Israel suffered substantial destruction from a tornado, Rabbi Levenson thanked the institutions "who responded with open hearts and outstretched arms" offering facilities and services. The list of Christian respondents to the disaster included Christian, Episcopal, Methodist, and Unitarian churches throughout Oklahoma City.[21]

At times the sympathy and support of Oklahoma Christians stretched to the Jews worldwide. Persons of good will responded to times of crisis for the Jew with funds and expressions of moral support. When the ritual murder trial of Mendel Beilis took place in Russia in 1913, Bishop Francis K. Brooke, an Episcopalian of Oklahoma, was among those who signed protests against the preposterous accusation. And when the war relief campaign to alleviate the tragic condition of Europe's Jews took place in 1917, the Reverend J. S. Murrow of Atoka joined it with a moving fervor that attracted the attention of Jews nationally. His letter read:

I am not a Jew—I am an old worn out Christian-Indian Missionary—a Baptist.
Your God is my God—Your Father my Father—Your people are my Master's people, your brethren are my brethren.
My means are small—but my heart greatly rejoices because of the privilege of sending the enclosed one hundred dollars for the relief of the suffering and starving Jews of Europe.[22]

The leaders of the Jewish War Relief Association, deeply impressed, reproduced one million copies of the letter for their campaign.

Although an institutional framework for interfaith work was not large, both Christian and Jew made accommodations to improve relations and understanding between the communities. Branches of the National Conference of Christians and Jews were created in Tulsa and Oklahoma City. In the late sixties clergy in Tulsa formed a Metropolitan Ministry to further contact. In Oklahoma City Rabbi Levenson constructed an Institute for Christian Clergy for the same purpose and to permit the opportunity for greater knowledge. Such interfaith efforts still occur frequently on a formal and informal basis.

Much more important and less dramatic than responses to specific crises, of course, is the quality of the relationships among the people living together. Christian and Jew alike attested to peaceful and harmonious relations as the ordinary condition of life. "Complete social acceptance within the non-Jewish community," wrote Rabbi Levenson in the mid-fifties of Enid, "is entirely possible for those Jews who seek it."[23] Christian residents of Enid made the same remarks to me; they were unaware of any invidious tensions or latent feelings of hostility. Mrs. Rose Grad, commenting on her life in Carnegie and her inclusion in the social activities of the town, noted that at times she lost awareness that she was Jewish.[24] And over and over the sentiments of Alfred Aaronson come through, that the friendliness and openness of the people made Tulsa a special city and inspired his own desire to give back to the community a measure of what it had given him.[25] In any measurement of anti-Semitism in Oklahoma against the spirit of friendliness and tolerance, much less observable in historical documents, perhaps, but much more intimately woven into the fabric of daily life, the friendliness has been by far the most impressive.

The contact between Jews and Christians offered by American life produced at least one kind of personal interaction extremely important to and controversial within the Jewish community—intermarriage. Intermarriage derived special significance for Oklahoma's Jews from their desire to maintain their identity though they were a small minority. A small group could find its very existence threatened by marriages which drew both the marriage partners and children away from the beliefs of and membership in the group.

General studies on intermarriage between American Jews and Christians reveal characteristics that apply as well to Oklahoma's Jews. To some extent the size of the group affects the incidence of intermarriage, although size alone is not a reliable guide. Jewish-gentile marriage, for instance, is quite low in New York, but quite high in other large cities, such as Washington, D. C. The latter, it appears, attracts many single young Jews. Jewish men intermarried more than Jewish women. Assimilated Jews did so more frequently than less assimilated ones. Nevertheless, in terms of community the small towns see and feel the effects of intermarriage the most.

As a public or communal issue, intermarriage could have no meaning before the creation of Jewish institutions. And even when it did become a matter of communal concern it remained essentially a private matter for the individual and the family. Under these circumstances we have little public indication of its meaning.

In Oklahoma, intermarriage has been an ever-present concern to Jews. From the first Jewish settlement to the present day their small numbers placed the Jews in social dependence upon the surrounding population. Young Jews had only a small population base on which to build their social lives if they chose to restrict themselves to Jewish friends and mates. In the smallest towns social relationships with Christians were the only possible social life outside the family. Even in Oklahoma City and Tulsa social contact with the majority population was constant in business, school, and other activities.

Intermarriage appears to have occurred rarely for the first-generation immigrants. Moreover, the continuous influx of first-generation immigrants before the First World War and the resultant rapid growth of Jewish population kept it at a low level. By the early thirties there is some evidence that the process of assimilation and intermarriage had become disturbing to some of the religious and communal leaders of the state. There were considerable efforts to produce an array of institutions to deal with the internal needs of the community and to prevent its being swamped from without. Even so, Max May, an important figure in the Tulsa Reform community, found Tulsa's efforts woefully inadequate and found the attempt a continual struggle for existence.[26] Rabbi Oscar Fasman of Tulsa's Orthodox B'nai Emunah congregation found it worthwhile to comment on the difficulties of the Jews in smaller communities who were scattered and unable to receive a proper Jewish education.[27] Rabbi Fasman also drew attention to the failure of Jewish boys to date Jewish girls in Tulsa as often as they might and should.[28] The topic must have been a frequent theme of discussion for it cut to the heart of Jewish survival.

The fear of intermarriage influenced the Jews to take measures against it. A variety of reasons induced the creation of Jewish fraternities and sororities at institutions of higher learning, particularly the University of Oklahoma. The threat of intermarriage played its part in the attempt to encourage social life and living conditions there within a Jewish context. Jewish families sometimes considered its possibility when they chose to move from smaller to larger communities where a larger Jewish population and institutional network enabled their children to grow up among Jewish children.

Intermarriage has continued to occur in Oklahoma as elsewhere in the country. It has not decimated the Jewish population of Oklahoma but has left open some nagging questions. Changing attitudes toward religious preference have led to considerable numbers of interfaith marriages in which the non-Jewish member affiliates with the Jewish community. On the other hand, the increased number of intermarriages may indicate a general weakening of religion as an important fact of life in the society. Some students of the phenomenon assume that under such circumstances Judaism would lose its distinctive character and be absorbed into the general culture.

From another point of view, however, the frequency of intermarriage is a normal result of the openness of American society and the acceptance of the Jews as equal members within it. Those who fear for the future existence of the Jewish population must invoke self-imposed barriers between the Jews and the gentiles to reduce its incidence. If they do not do so, they must hope that those who intermarry will turn to Judaism rather be neutral or adopt other faiths. The latter two courses will separate the children from the faith of the grandparents at the very least. Without doubt, however, the factor of interfaith marriage remains a private affair in which parents and children possess both the problems and the answers. The community can only play a secondary role in resolving it.

Chapter 5

THE RECENT PERIOD

From the middle of the fifties the population trend in Oklahoma reversed itself, taking an upward swing. From the low point of 2,210,000 in 1955 it rose to 2,567,000 in 1970 and has continued to grow since. And as if to prove the proposition that as Oklahoma's population goes so goes its Jewish population, the number of Jews in the state also increased. From a low point of 4,750 in 1955 their numbers rose to 6,480 by 1970, almost where it had been forty-three years earlier in 1927.

While both the state and the Jewish population made modest comebacks, their growth remained unimpressive by national standards. Oklahoma's rank among the states declined from twenty-sixth to twenty-seventh place while the rank of its Jewish population dropped correspondingly from thirty-sixth to thirty-seventh place between the mid-fifties and the mid-seventies. But even as America's Jewish population continued to grow in this generation, it was slowly becoming a smaller part of the total population. That fact distinguishes the post–World War II era from the earlier period.

Within the state, the pattern of increased urban development continued. Fifty-one percent of Oklahoma's population in 1950 was urban; in 1970 that proportion had risen to 68 percent. By 1970 Tulsa and Oklahoma City accounted for over 37 percent of the total population of the state and well over half of its urban population. And Oklahoma's Jewish population followed suit. Over 60 percent of the Jews in the state resided in the two cities in 1972 compared with 46 percent in 1927. Tulsa, with 2,500, led the way, while Oklahoma City, followed with 1,500. The Jewish population of the two cities, however, had not changed markedly from their 1927 levels.

The smaller towns of the state scarcely maintained their Jewish population, declined, or, in the case of extremely small numbers, lost all of their Jews. In the early seventies only Muskogee of the early places of Jewish settlement, with 120 in its Jewish community, still possessed over 100 Jews. As the decade of the seventies neared its end even Muskogee appeared to be in increasing difficulty. "There are so few Jewish people remaining," a communal leader wrote in 1979, "that we no longer have religious school for youngsters."[1]

Sadly, but perhaps inevitably, the towns with the smallest Jewish populations dropped out of the column of places with Jewish residents. The Grad family, the sole family of Carnegie (with the exception of a single male) sold their Dixie store, a local landmark, after Mr. Grad died in 1965. Mrs. Grad, who had lived there since her arrival in America in 1922, then moved to Oklahoma City to be near her daughter. Similarly, the Levite family, whose store in Apache had celebrated its seventieth anniversary in 1973, ended its existence in the town with the death of George Levite a short time after that date. His children had departed, one living in Norman and the second out of state. Clearly, greener pastures were drawing the younger generation out of the smaller towns. The children were often well-educated and sought careers and lives that did not include following in the parents' footsteps, sometimes with the blessing of their parents.

The Apaches and Carnegies did not present the whole picture of the smaller towns in the recent period. New or even continuing developments produced new needs which led to growth in other communities. In the second half of the seventies, Norman's growth included enough Jewish population to qualify as the third largest concentration in the state. The B'nai Brith directory for 1977–78 reported about 140 adult Jews in the city.[2] A significant portion of them served either on the faculty of the university directly or within the university community in some capacity.

The appearance of a sizable Jewish community in Norman with a large element of professionals, added an important new dimension for Oklahoma Jewry. This was most discernible in Norman for the town was atypical of the state in its character. The sharp rise in university attendance and in graduate study nationwide after the Second World War witnessed a corresponding increase in the numbers of Jewish faculty members in higher education across the country. Oklahoma shared in this phenomenon. Writing in the early mid-fifties, Rabbi Levenson found "about a half-dozen Jews" on the Norman campus faculty.[3] In the middle seventies there were several score Jewish faculty.

The pattern of Jewish economic life in the larger cities has also changed in the last generation. National trends in marketing have modified and placed at some disadvantage earlier types of enterprises, changes already discernible in the twenties and thirties. The small store, although still important, has given way before the chain store and the shopping center has displaced, or provided very heavy competition for, central downtown areas.

Although some of the Jewish chains survived and prospered, others declined for business or family reasons. Such chains as the Sanditen family's Oklahoma Tire and Supply Company illustrates continuity, but of the May Brothers clothing stores only one remains. Milton May, who joined his father's firm in the twenties, closed the downtown Oklahoma City store in the early seventies, a response to the program of urban renewal undertaken in the city. He then retired after closing another store in a fashionable shopping center. Sylvan Goldman, who owned the Humpty Dumpty grocery chain in the thirties, went on to the manufacture of grocery carts and a variety of other interests. Community activists in Tulsa recently were unable to recall whether a single Jewish grocery store still existed in the city.[4] As a result of some of these changes the character of Jewish participation in the mercantile world has been altered. Jews become executives rather than storefront proprietors in both family and non-family enterprises.

Another sign of change lies in the increasing numbers engaged in the professions. Although there were Jewish doctors and lawyers in the twenties, by the seventies their proportion of the Jewish occupational force had increased markedly. The seventy-fifth anniversary booklet of Temple B'nai Israel disclosed that nearly one-fifth of the membership was part of the legal and medical professions. With the membership which had been in the community for twenty-five years or more as a comparison, the two professions would have amounted to about 13 percent in the early fifties.[5] Tulsans likewise assumed that the number of professionals had risen in their community in recent decades.

Oklahoma's Jews have gradually departed from the early forms of frontier and small town entrepreneurship. The changes, whether dictated by personal and familial factors or larger economic and social forces in society, indicate both a capacity and a willingness on the part of the Jews to adapt to new circumstances in the state. The bulk of Oklahoma's Jewish population, surprisingly stable in a society where movement of people is an accepted fact of life, indi-

Henry J. Tobias

cates perhaps more than any other single fact the success and basic satisfaction of Oklahoma's Jews with their experience in the state. Ben Byers, a pioneer of the Jewish community in Oklahoma, stated it simply and aptly: "My children were all born and educated in Oklahoma and I have never regretted leaving the old country and coming to a country of much freedom and many opportunities."[6]

Today the Jews of Oklahoma remain a vital community, though their numbers remain small. In their larger communities they retain a strong identity although they seek, as always, to integrate with the general population among whom they reside. The economic and social character of the Jewish population is changing, as is the character of the state itself. Oklahoma's Jews are adapting to meet the general changes in society while they seek to remain integrated and to retain their identity.

The settlement of the Jews in Oklahoma matched the growth of the state, even to the point of declining when the state's population declined. Only in recent years have these parallel trends altered slightly with the Jewish population failing to keep pace with the state's renewed growth. The major reason for this change may well lie in the character of Jewish economic and social life, which is heavily middle class in the state. Bearing relatively few children, the Jewish population may simply not be renewing itself. In earlier generations immigration, foreign and from other states, kept the state's Jewish population growing. When Jewish immigration fell, so did the relative proportion of the Jews to the whole population. In this sense, the declining Jewish population of Oklahoma matches the declining percentage of the Jewish population in American society.

Such trends may not be permanent. Although a sizable new wave of Jewish immigration to the United States seems unlikely, population shifts within the country are possible and, indeed, are taking place. Oklahoma's regional position as a developing economy could still attract newcomers by offering better opportunities than other parts of the country. If so, some of that new population will be Jewish. Even if a decline continued in the relative weight of the Jewish population in the country, there might still be a renewed growth of Jewish population in the state. But there is little reason to anticipate a large influx of Jews into Oklahoma.

The small size of the Jewish population in the state has affected them in several ways. It has led them to create a surprisingly full network of institutions to enable them to maintain their identity. It also has resulted in a strong degree of external assimilation.

69

While their contribution to the general civic welfare has been proportionately greater than their numbers, few Jews have run for political office in Oklahoma. They do not appear as a political bloc in any formal sense, although political candidates have appealed to them as a group occasionally. The reasons probably lie partly in the peculiarities of individual character but they may also indicate a sense of insecurity, of not wishing to attract attention in any public competitive sense.

The Jewish community, by virtues of its assimilative push, has lost most traces of ethnicity. Its own strong internal institutional character, however, supports Jewish identity in faith and in concern for Jews elsewhere. Strong ties of kinship within the state bind many together as well. The internal solidity expressed in these factors contributes to the stability of the group. It is not torn by sharp differences among the congregations. Moreover, the long-standing ties many of the residents have to each other provide a powerful impetus for continued existence.

In their economic pursuits, the Jews of Oklahoma have gradually become more akin to the surrounding population. In part this trend is the result of their adaptation to changes occurring in the economy and in part, it is a result of the economy changing in the direction of the traditional pursuits of the Jews. The Jews remain committed to mercantile pursuits in accord with their age-old experience. There are, however, fewer individual stores, more Jewish executives in larger businesses, more Jews in the professions and in social services. The economic growth and urbanization of Oklahoma have made business more important in the state and have increased the number of Oklahomans engaged in it. In this sense, the Jew has become less distinctive than before and is perhaps somewhat less visible in the population.

For a century Jews have lived in Oklahoma. Their roots are as deep as those of any group that settled here outside of the native Americans. They have given and continue to give much to the state and they receive much in return. The experience of the Jews in the United States generally has been one of the happier chapters of Jewish history in modern times. That segment of their experience that unfolds in Oklahoma partakes of the same satisfying quality and allows hope for the future.

Chapter 6

BIBLIOGRAPHICAL ESSAY

The study of Jewish history in Oklahoma involves acquaintance with a wide range of information. In its broadest perspective, the history of the Jews in the state cannot be understood apart from their general history, from the history of the state itself. In this sense even general works related to these topics contain considerable information for comprehending the background and context of the problems and development of Oklahoma's Jews.

General works on European and American history exist in large numbers with new editions and studies appearing constantly and available in all libraries. Less known to the general reader are some of the important works about Jewish history. The outstanding figures of modern Jewish historiography are Simon Dubnow, whose five-volume *History of the Jews* (New York: Thomas Yoseloff, 1967–73) brought the subject matter into line with modern thought, and Salo W. Baron, whose sixteen volumes on the *Social and Religious History of the Jews* (Philadelphia: The Jewish Publication Society of America, 1952–76), went far to complete what Dubnow had begun. A basic reference tool to add to these interpretive works is the *Encyclopedia Judaica*, edited by Cecil Roth and Geoffrey Wigoder (New York: Macmillan, 1972) in sixteen volumes. Almost any topic dealing with the long history of the Jews receives some mention in the above works.

Information on the Jews in America exists in large quantities. Several of the best known surveys include Oscar Handlin's *Adventure in Freedom* (New York: McGraw Hill, 1954) and the fourth volume of *The Jewish People: Past and Present* (New York: Jewish Encyclopedic Handbooks, 1955). The latter volume contains long articles which offer valuable background materials for the student and serious researcher. More recent works of a sociological character include

Marshall Sklare's *America's Jews* (New York: Random House, 1971) and Oscar I. Janowsky's edited work, *The American Jew* (Philadelphia: The Jewish Publication Society of America, 1964). The greatest single continuing source of information exists in the compiled data, scholarly articles, and news items of the *American Jewish Year Book* which has appeared annually under the direction of the American Jewish Committee since 1900.

The list of monographic works of a thematic nature is long and varied. Leonard Dinnerstein's edited volume of articles, *Antisemitism in the United States* (New York: Holt, Rinehart and Winston, 1971) contains a variety of interpretations on this important subject. John Higham's *Strangers in the Land* (New York: Atheneum, 1973) examines the sources of American nativism primarily in relation to the Jew up to 1925. An interesting context for understanding Oklahoma's Jews can be found in Leonard Dinnerstein's and Mary Dale Palsson's edited work, *Jews in the South* (Baton Rouge: Louisiana State University Press, 1973). These volumes contain many suggestions for further reading.

There are many periodicals and collections which contain articles, source materials, or are themselves sources for the history of the Jews in Oklahoma directly or have information which can be gleaned from materials not directly touching upon Jewish history. The *Southwest Jewish Chronicle,* published in Oklahoma City since 1929, and the *Tulsa Jewish Review,* which has been coming out since 1930, offer a mass of material for Jewish history in Oklahoma as well as articles about Jews generally. The *Chronicles of Oklahoma* contains a range of articles covering the spectrum of Oklahoma history with materials included on Jewish families and individuals. The "Indian-Pioneer Papers," gathered in the 1930s on the basis of interviews with long-term residents, holds many nuggets of otherwise unobtainable information. Copies exist at the State Historical Society and in the Western History Collections at the University of Oklahoma. In addition, the *Western States Jewish Historical Quarterly,* published since 1968, has materials on the Jews in the West.

The history of Oklahoma, too, has attracted the efforts of many researchers. Some of the older so-called mug histories contain detailed information on the early development of the state and numerous biographies of leading figures. John D. Benedict's *History of Muskogee and Northeast Oklahoma* in three volumes (Chicago: S. J. Clarke Publishing Co., 1922) and Joseph B. Thoburn and Muriel H. Wright's five-volume *Oklahoma: A History of the State and Its*

People (New York: Lewis Historical Publishing Co., 1929), are typical of the genre. More modern single-volume works of merit include Arrell M. Gibson's *Oklahoma: A History of Five Centuries* (Norman: Harlow Publishing Company, 1965), and H. Wayne and Anne Hodges Morgan's *Oklahoma: A Bicentennial History* (New York: Norton, 1977).

Very few detailed works exist on the Jews in Oklahoma. One of them is Terry P. Wilson's *Wheeling Carts Round the World: The Career of Sylvan N. Goldman* (Norman: University of Oklahoma Press, 1978). However, there are many types of materials for the imaginative researcher which could add to our knowledge of the subject matter. The footnotes of the text reveal only a few of these. In addition, it may be pointed out that a major, barely tapped resource lies in the living persons whose recollections still cover a significant portion of the total history of the Jews in the state. The information they could supply would probably more than match the materials which exist in print.

NOTES

CHAPTER 1

1. U. S., Congress, Senate, Reports of the Immigration Commission, *Emigration Conditions in Europe,* 61st Congress, 3d Session, v. 4, p. 57.

2. Nathan Glazer, "Social Characteristics of American Jews, 1654–1954," *American Jewish Year Book* (New York: The American Jewish Committee, 1955), v. 56, p. 9.

3. *Ibid.,* p. 11.

CHAPTER 2

1. Randall M. Falk, "A History of the Jews of Oklahoma with special emphasis on the Tulsa Jewish Community" (Rabbinical thesis, Hebrew Union College, 1946), p. 12.

2. *American Jewish Year Book* (Philadelphia: The Jewish Publication Society of America, 1901), v. 3, p. 147. The *Year Book* was the major source of information on American Jews.

3. Cited in Charles I. Cooper, "The Story of the Jews of Oklahoma," *The Oklahoma Jewish Chronicle,* 1, (December, 1929), 4.

4. U. S., Bureau of the Census, *Census of Religious Bodies, 1936. Jewish Congregations: Statistics, History, Doctrine and Organization* (Washington: GPO, 1940), p. 4.

5. Cited in John D. Benedict, *Muskogee and Northeastern Oklahoma* (Chicago: The S. J. Clarke Publishing Company, 1922), v. 2, pp. 179, 339–42.

6. Gaston L. Litton, *History of Oklahoma* (New York: Lewis Historical Publishing Co., 1957), v. 3, pp. 521–22.

7. Works Progress Administration, "Indian-Pioneer Papers," Western History Collections, The University of Oklahoma, v. 14, pp. 292–94.

8. Martin Zofness, "Address to the Washington County Historical Society," (n. p.) April 17, 1974.

9. Oscar and Mary Handlin, "A Century of Jewish Immigration to the United States," *American Jewish Year Book* (New York: The American Jewish Committee, 1950), v. 50, p. 14.

10. *American Jewish Year Book* (Philadelphia: The Jewish Publication Society of America, 1918), v. 20, p. 71.

11. Cited in Litton, *History of Oklahoma,* v. 4, p. 521.

12. "Indian-Pioneer Papers," v. 29, p. 47.

13. Southwestern Bell Telephone Company, *Economic Survey of Oklahoma* (St. Louis, 1929), p. 137.

14. Frederick L. Ryan, *The Rehabilitation of Oklahoma Coal Mining Communities* (Norman: University of Oklahoma Press, 1935), p. 31.

15. *The Standard Blue Book of Oklahoma, 1910–11* (Oklahoma City: A. J. Peeler and Co., 1909), p. 186.

16. Grace Goldin, "I Remember Tulsa," *Commentary on the American Scene,* ed. Eliot E. Cohen (New York: Knopf, 1953), p. 43.

17. Falk, "The Jews of Oklahoma," p. 36.

18. Rabbi Joseph Levenson, "The Story of Oklahoma Jewry" (Unpublished manuscript, [1953?]), p. 6.

19. Interview with Mrs. Rose Grad, Oklahoma City, February 19, 1979.

20. Gary Watters, "The Russian Jew in Oklahoma: The May Brothers," *The Chronicles of Oklahoma,* 53 (Winter, 1975–76), 499; interview with Mr. Milton May, Oklahoma City, March 12, 1979.

21. *Tulsa Jewish Review,* v. 3, no. 7, (September, 1932), p. 2.

22. Levenson, "Oklahoma Jewry," p. 11.

23. *Ibid.*

CHAPTER 3

1. U. S., Bureau of the Census, *Census of Religious Bodies, 1926. Jewish Congregations: Statistics, History, Doctrine and Organization* (Washington: GPO, 1929), p. 17.

2. Cited in Joseph L. Blau, "The Spiritual Life of American Jewry, 1654–1954," *American Jewish Year Book,* (New York: The American Jewish Committee, 1955), v. 56, p. 105.

3. Jacob Agus, "Current Movements in the Religious Life of American Jewry," *The Jewish People: Past and Present,* v. 4 (New York: Jewish Encyclopedic Handbooks, 1955), p. 128.

4. *Ibid.*

5. Falk, "The Jews of Oklahoma," p. 9.

6. Benedict, *Muskogee,* v. 2, p. 160.

7. *Ibid.,* v. 2, p. 343.

8. Falk, "The Jews of Oklahoma," pp. 10–11.

9. Emanuel Men's Club, *This is Emanuel,* 1970, (n. p.), p. 2.

10. *Tulsa Jewish Review,* v. 1, no. 7, (September, 1930), p. 3.

11. Interview with Mrs. Jenny Brouse, March 14, 1979; Tulsa Jewish Community Council Tape, Mr. Henry Fist, 1976.

12. Cited in Philip Friedman, "Political and Social Movements and Organizations," *The Jewish People: Past and Present* (New York: Jewish Encyclopedic Handbooks, 1955), v. 4, p. 144.

13. Cited *ibid.,* p. 150.

14. *American Jewish Year Book* (Philadelphia: The Jewish Publication Society of America, 1906), v. 8, pp. 218, 220.

15. Cited in Friedman, *The Jewish People: Past and Present,* v. 4, p. 147.

Henry J. Tobias

16. Cited *ibid.*, p. 155.
17. Levenson, "Oklahoma Jewry," p. 4.
18. *The Oklahoma Jewish Chronicle,* v. 1, no. 1, (December, 1929), p. 10.
19. *Tulsa Jewish Review,* v. 1, no. 2, (April, 1930), p. 3.
20. *The Oklahoma Jewish Chronicle,* v. 1, no. 1, (December, 1929), p. 12.
21. *The Southwest Jewish Chronicle* (June, 1975), pp. 10, 20.

CHAPTER 4

1. "Indian-Pioneer Papers," v. 104, p. 515; and v. 9, pp. 87–89.
2. *Ibid.,* v. 24, p. 362.
3. Falk, "The Jews of Oklahoma," p. 33.
4. Angelo C. Scott, *The Story of Oklahoma City* (Oklahoma City: Times-Journal Publishing Co., 1939), p. 185.
5. Falk, "The Jews of Oklahoma," p. 34.
6. Oscar Handlin, "American Views of the Jew at the Opening of the Twentieth Century," *Antisemitism in the United States,* ed. Leonard Dinnerstein (New York: Holt, Rinehart and Winston, 1971), p. 55.
7. John Higham, "American Antisemitism Historically Reconsidered," *ibid.,* p. 74.
8. *Tulsa Daily World,* July 14, 1922, p. 4.
9. *Proceedings of the Constitutional Convention of the Proposed State of Oklahoma Held at Guthrie, Oklahoma, November 20, 1906 to November 16, 1907* (Muskogee, Oklahoma: Muskogee Printing Co., [1907?]), pp. 73, 115.
10. *American Jewish Year Book* (Philadelphia: The Jewish Publication Society of America, 1907), v. 9, p. 554.
11. *Guthrie Daily Leader,* November 1, 1912, p. 1.
12. Cited in *Oklahoma Jewish Chronicle,* v. 1, no. 1, p. 6.
13. Watters, *The Chronicles of Oklahoma,* 53 (Winter, 1975–76), 488–89.
14. *The Daily Oklahoman,* March 26, 1921, p. 4.
15. Letter to J. F. May, March 27, 1921. Milton May, Oklahoma City.
16. Letter to May Brothers, March 31, 1921. Milton May, Oklahoma City.
17. Letter to May Brothers, April 4, 1921. Milton May, Oklahoma City.
18. Carter Blue Clark, "A History of the Ku Klux Klan in Oklahoma" (Ph.D. dissertation, University of Oklahoma, 1976), p. 161.
19. *Ibid.,* p. 90.
20. Keith L. Bryant, Jr., *Alfalfa Bill Murray* (Norman: University of Oklahoma Press, 1968), p. 271.
21. Cited in *An Evening of Celebration, Temple B'nai Israel, 1903–78.*
22. Cited in *Oklahoma Jewish Chronicle,* v. 2, no. 3, (April, 1930), p. 13.
23. Levenson, "Oklahoma Jewry," p. 8.
24. Interview with Mrs. Rose Grad, Oklahoma City, February 19, 1979.
25. Tulsa Jewish Community Council Tape, Alfred Aaronson, 1976.
26. *Tulsa Jewish Review,* v. 1, no. 7, (September, 1930), p. 13.
27. *Ibid.,* v. 1, no. 11, (January, 1931), p. 8.
28. *Ibid.,* v. 2, no. 10, (December, 1931), p. 16.

CHAPTER 5

1. Letter from Norman Miskin, president of Beth Ahaba, to Mrs. E. F. Friedman, March 20, 1979. Mrs. E. F. Friedman, Oklahoma City.

2. B'nai Brith, Louis Berlowitz Lodge No. 539, *1977–78 Community Directory,* Oklahoma City, Oklahoma.

3. Levenson, "Oklahoma Jewry," p. 9a.

4. Interview with Mrs. Jenny Brouse, Tulsa, March 14, 1979.

5. *An Evening of Celebration, Temple B'nai Israel, 1903–78.*

6. "Indian-Pioneer Papers," v. 14, p. 294.